PRAISE FOR

DON'T GIVE THE ENEMY A SEAT AT YOUR TABLE

May 2021

Louie writes with hope and speaks freedom to our weary hearts that need the victory available to us through Jesus. This book is **a treasure you'll return to again and again**. I can't wait for you to read it and see your life transformed!

LYSA TERKEURST

#1 *NEW YORK TIMES* BESTSELLING AUTHOR AND PRESIDENT OF PROVERBS 31 MINISTRIES

All of us know what it's like to feel trapped in endless loops of self-defeating thoughts and the frustration of not knowing how to interrupt the circuit on them. This wise and practical book provides the guidance we need to **break free from the tyranny of negative thinking** and reclaim joy. Highly recommended!

IAN MORGAN CRON

AUTHOR OF *THE ROAD BACK TO YOU*

Louie Giglio is a prophetic gift for our time. And Psalm 23 is a resounding truth for all time. Put them together and you have **a clarion call to attune our mindstream** to life in the kingdom. As someone who starts every morning by praying Psalm 23, this book struck a deep chord in my heart.

JOHN MARK COMER

PASTOR OF VISION & TEACHING AT BRIDGETOWN CHURCH AND AUTHOR OF *THE RUTHLESS ELIMINATION OF HURRY*

Louie's new book, *Don't Give the Enemy a Seat at Your Table*, is **for anyone who's been letting the enemy occupy space** in their mind. Whether it's anger, loneliness, insecurity, or shame, it's time to kick the enemy out of your mind and take back your seat at the table.

STEVEN FURTICK

PASTOR OF ELEVATION CHURCH AND *NEW YORK TIMES* BESTSELLING AUTHOR

If you are wrestling with discouraging thoughts, pastor Louie Giglio's book, *Don't Give the Enemy a Seat at Your Table*, will help you **discover the biblical truths that will help free your mind** so you can live the life God intended you to live.

CRAIG GROESCHEL

PASTOR OF LIFE.CHURCH AND *NEW YORK TIMES* BESTSELLING AUTHOR

The greatest war of our lives centers around the battle of the mind. I am grateful for work like this that **floods our spiritual artillery with gospel ammunition**. Thank you, Louie G (that's the rap name I gave him), for giving us the kind of depth and accessibility we need to hold the line for the glory of God in the war zone of our minds.

KB

ARTIST

In the banquet of your heart there are two seats—one for you and the other for Jesus—and three is a crowd. That is the paradigm-shifting message of this important book, *Don't Give the Enemy a Seat at Your Table*. To the extent that you allow the devil to tag along and be a third wheel in your thought life, you will be derailed from your destiny. Let Louie show you how to **tell the enemy, "Seats taken," and you will watch your life change**.

LEVI AND JENNIE LUSKO

LEAD PASTORS OF FRESH LIFE CHURCH AND BESTSELLING AUTHORS

I'm confident that *Don't Give the Enemy a Seat at Your Table* will **not only clarify your faith but strengthen it**. Jesus has already won the greatest victory—now it's our turn to fight to think rightly and fix our eyes on our Good Shepherd.

TIM TEBOW

PROFESSIONAL ATHLETE AND SEC NATION COMMENTATOR, AUTHOR, KEYNOTE SPEAKER, AND PHILANTHROPIST

Don't Give the Enemy a Seat at Your Table is a gift! This wonderful book shows us how to access and exercise the resources we have in Christ so that we can **restore peace and rest to our minds**.

DR. CRAWFORD W. LORITTS, JR.

AUTHOR, SPEAKER, RADIO HOST, AND SENIOR PASTOR OF FELLOWSHIP BIBLE CHURCH

Don't Give the Enemy a Seat at Your Table is **a reflection and outpouring of fire-forged resolve and wisdom**, accompanied by the grace-gift of the tools Louie has been able to so practically articulate.

BROOKE AND SCOTT LIGERTWOOD

Don't Give the Enemy a Seat at Your Table reminds us of the identity that we have in Christ—that every battle He has won we have won also! Louie **shows us how God invites us into relationship** with Him and gives us a seat at His table, all the while winning the battle of your mind.

CHRISTIAN AND SADIE HUFF

Don't Give the Enemy a Seat at Your Table is **a world-changing, paradigm-shifting message** straight from Scripture.

EARL MCCLELLAN

PASTOR OF SHORELINE CITY CHURCH

Don't Give the Enemy a Seat at Your Table will equip you with practical tools to **align your thoughts with God's truth** so that you can fulfill your God-given purpose with passion and joy.

CHRISTINE CAINE

BESTSELLING AUTHOR
AND FOUNDER OF A21
AND PROPEL WOMEN

Don't Give the Enemy a Seat at Your Table is **undoubtedly a "now" word for this season, full of truth and encouragement** to help you take back every inch of ground the enemy has stolen from you and fully step into the peace, freedom, and victory Jesus died to give you.

CODY CARNES AND KARI JOBE CARNES

GRAMMY-NOMINATED
WORSHIP ARTISTS

There are few voices in Christendom who are able to **speak so pointedly to the realities** of the spiritual life. These pages are not just inspiration; they are preparation to do battle with darkness!

JOHN LINDELL

LEAD PASTOR OF
JAMES RIVER CHURCH
AND AUTHOR OF
SOUL SET FREE

Don't Give the Enemy a Seat at Your Table is **a triumphant guide** to finding the transformational hope sought by every hurting heart.

KATHERINE AND JAY WOLF

BESTSELLING AUTHORS
OF *SUFFER STRONG*
AND *HOPE HEALS*

DON'T
GIVE
THE ENEMY
A SEAT
AT YOUR
TABLE

ALSO BY LOUIE GIGLIO

Never Too Far

Not Forsaken

Goliath Must Fall

The Comeback

Waiting Here for You

Indescribable

I Am Not But I Know I Am

The Air I Breathe

CHILDREN'S BOOKS

Goliath Must Fall for Young Readers

*How Great Is Our God: 100 Indescribable
Devotions About God & Science*

Indescribable: 100 Devotions About God & Science

Indescribable for Little Ones

DON'T GIVE THE ENEMY A SEAT AT YOUR TABLE

IT'S TIME TO WIN THE BATTLE OF YOUR MIND . . .

LOUIE GIGLIO

W PUBLISHING GROUP

AN IMPRINT OF THOMAS NELSON

Published in Nashville, Tennessee, by W Publishing, an imprint of Thomas Nelson.

Thomas Nelson titles may be purchased in bulk for educational, business, fundraising, or sales promotional use. For information, please email SpecialMarkets@ThomasNelson.com.

Unless otherwise noted, Scripture quotations are taken from the Holy Bible, New International Version®, NIV®. Copyright © 1973, 1978, 1984, 2011 by Biblica, Inc.® Used by permission of Zondervan. All rights reserved worldwide. www.zondervan.com. The "NIV" and "New International Version" are trademarks registered in the United States Patent and Trademark Office by Biblica, Inc.®

Scripture quotations marked BSB are from the Holy Bible, Berean Study Bible, BSB. Copyright © 2016, 2020 by Bible Hub. Used by permission. All rights reserved worldwide.

Scripture quotations marked ESV are from the ESV Bible® (The Holy Bible, English Standard Version®), copyright © 2001 by Crossway, a publishing ministry of Good News Publishers. Used by permission. All rights reserved.

Scripture quotations marked GNT are from the Good News Translation in Today's English Version— Second Edition. Copyright © 1992 by American Bible Society. Used by permission.

Scripture quotations marked THE MESSAGE are taken from *The Message*. Copyright © 1993, 2002, 2018 by Eugene H. Peterson. Used by permission of NavPress. All rights reserved. Represented by Tyndale House Publishers, Inc.

Scripture quotations marked NASB are from the New American Standard Bible® (NASB®), Copyright © 1960, 1971, 1977, 1995, 2020 by The Lockman Foundation. Used by permission. All rights reserved. www.Lockman.org.

Scripture quotations marked NKJV are from the New King James Version®. Copyright © 1982 by Thomas Nelson. Used by permission. All rights reserved.

Scripture quotations marked NLT are taken from the Holy Bible, New Living Translation. Copyright © 1996, 2004, 2015 by Tyndale House Foundation. Used by permission of Tyndale House Publishers, Inc., Carol Stream, Illinois 60188. All rights reserved.

Any internet addresses, phone numbers, or company or product information printed in this book are offered as a resource and are not intended in any way to be or to imply an endorsement by Thomas Nelson, nor does Thomas Nelson vouch for the existence, content, or services of these sites, phone numbers, companies, or products beyond the life of this book.

ISBN 978-0-7852-4736-4 (audiobook)
ISBN 978-0-7852-4734-0 (eBook)
ISBN 978-0-7852-4722-7 (HC)

Library of Congress Cataloging-in-Publication Data

Library of Congress Control Number: 2020952512

Printed in the United States of America

21 22 23 24 25 LSC 10 9 8 7 6 5 4 3 2 1

Be grateful for the storms in life.
They reveal who your true friends are.
To the friend who sent the text that has
become the title of this book—
thank you for allowing God to use you to change my life.

CONTENTS

NINE WORDS THAT WILL CHANGE YOUR LIFE

I felt attacked. Misrepresented. Abandoned. Wounded.

Shelley and I were in the midst of a massive storm—one of the toughest seasons we've ever faced as leaders. Darts were flying at me from every direction. My heart was heavy and conflicted.

The moment we had decided years ago to plant a local church, a friend was chillingly clear in his assessment of the journey we were embarking on: *It will be the hardest thing you've ever done.*

At the time, I brushed those words aside. *We've done some pretty difficult things*, I thought. But now, his words echoed in my mind. He was right. Building a kingdom family called the "local church" out of a tribe of mostly strangers was exposing my optimism (I thought we'd never have insider struggles like every other church), and, even at fifty years of age, I was facing challenges that were testing the limits of my experience.

Now the insider struggles were real. Intense. Personal. Bitterness and frustration worked overtime to get a foothold in my spirit. More than once I wondered if it was worth it and wanted to pack it in and quit.

One evening, a few months into that tumultuous stretch, I found myself at the top of our driveway furiously working away on a text message to a friend I could trust. Earlier in the afternoon I had found out about something that vindicated my case. I've always believed in the saying *You don't have to tell your side of the story; time will.* On this day it felt like time was telling the world that I was right, and obviously I wasn't going to sit on good news. I wanted other people to know I was right too. So I reached out to someone who had stood with me in the struggle, someone who had taken a few shots on my behalf.

Wow... what a text it was. A lengthy masterpiece of angst and vindication, the tone of which went something like this: *You're not gonna believe what just happened. I'm not saying I was right, but hey, it is what it is! Can you believe it? I mean, if you give things enough time, you'll see people's true colors, right? I mean, finally... blah, blah, blah.*

I pressed send and waited. Literally. I just stared at the screen, looking for support to arrive. I wanted a reply that resounded with a hearty, *Hey, Louie, I've got your back! I knew you were right all along!* I wanted a shoulder to cry on. A celebratory high five or fist bump (*not* the emoji kind). I needed actual words in return, and lots of them.

A moment passed. Another. I waited.

Let's pause for a moment and let the focus swing to *your* story.

Have you ever sent a text like that?

You don't need to be planting a church to be in a hard place. Everybody experiences tense circumstances where your mind is heavy and you feel like you're under attack. Times when you want to swing big and fight back or you want to give up. What do you do?

How do you win the battle of your mind?

THE TEXT THAT CHANGED EVERYTHING

When you're in a hard stretch filled with conflict and confusion, if you could just get your thoughts in order you could probably figure out a way to proceed, but keeping a clear head is more difficult than it sounds.

Maybe you're on the wrong side of someone else's harmful

actions or hurtful words. Maybe the conflict comes from within. You feel abandoned. Falsely attacked. Hurt. Defeated. Tempted. Lost. Your mood is low. Your mind is stressed. You're weary from the endless conversations you're having inside your head with friends, coworkers, family members, accusers. Conversations where you're always vindicated and their faults are exposed.

It's easy at those times for fear or despair to set in. You find yourself constantly looking over your shoulder, wondering if someone's out to get you. You struggle with your emotions. You snap in anger. You break down in tears. It's not uncommon to give in to those dark thoughts, especially when you're staring at the ceiling at two in the morning, desperately trying to take control of the narrative and manage the outcome. You feel like your back is against the wall, and paranoia can become your unshakable companion. You keep your defenses high.

And you seek allies. You look for someone—anyone—who sees things your way. You gravitate toward anyone who will hear your side of the story and commiserate with you. That's the position I was in standing outside my house fixated on that little circle spinning around on my phone, indicating a reply to my text was on the way.

Remember, I needed my friend's reply to be commensurate with the effort that went into my message. I was anxious for something beefy and bold. Lots of affirmation and solidarity. Lots of words.

And then it arrived. A one-sentence reply. Nine words to be exact. In dismay I blurted, "You've got to be kidding!" But when I leaned in and focused on the message, those nine words changed my life. The message read:

Don't give the Enemy a seat at your table.

I pushed aside my annoyance and let the message sink in. Quickly I saw that my friend had nailed it. I had allowed my adversary—the Devil—to influence the conversation inside my mind.

My struggle wasn't about fighting with people. People were involved, but the battle I was facing was against principalities and powers of darkness (Ephesians 6:12). My heavenly Father wasn't making me afraid or paranoid. My Shepherd wasn't putting thoughts of despair in my mind. The harmful thoughts were coming from someone else.

The Enemy had taken a seat at my table, and I was allowing myself to listen to a killer. Right there in my driveway, I determined to take back my table. The Devil would have to flee.

In the days that followed, my mind was riveted on those nine words. As negative thoughts would enter my mind, I'd say to myself, *Don't give the Enemy a seat. Don't entertain his ideas. These thoughts are not from a good and trustworthy Shepherd. Move on.*

Soon after, I was led to study Psalm 23—a text that has

THE ENEMY
HAD TAKEN A
SEAT AT MY
TABLE, AND I
WAS ALLOWING
MYSELF TO
LISTEN TO
A KILLER.

———————————

comforted and steadied God's people through the ages as they have navigated troubled waters. Now I was seeing it through fresh eyes. Especially the line that reads, "You prepare a table before me in the presence of my enemies" (v. 5).

I could see myself sitting at a table, with the Good Shepherd across from me. He had led me through dark valleys to reach the table, and I didn't need to be afraid, even though the fiery trials weren't all resolved. My place at the table didn't mean that my enemies would be removed from the equation. In fact, the table was set right in the middle of my enemies. That captivated my imagination and held my attention.

I didn't need to vindicate myself. I didn't need to clear my name. I didn't need to control this equation or work overtime to improve it. My task was to concentrate on the Good Shepherd, the One who owned the table.

My invitation was to put my trust in the One who prompted me to lie down in green pastures, the One who led me beside quiet waters and restored my soul. The Good Shepherd was guiding me along the right paths for His name's sake. Dark valleys and hard times were part of those paths, yet He would be with me and see me through every threatening night. The Good Shepherd would anoint my life with His favor and my cup would overflow. My promise—goodness, mercy, and love—would escort me every single day of my life.

My destiny was set. I didn't need to be afraid. The Shepherd was at the table, and He would see to it that I was going to dwell in the house of the Lord forever.

Day after day I sat with the truth of Psalm 23, letting it burrow its way into my soul. From 1 Peter 5:8, I knew that a major tactic of the Devil was to prowl around my life. So maybe I couldn't stop the Devil from prowling around my table, but in Jesus' name I definitely did have the choice whether I allowed the Enemy to sit down.

God's Word was transforming my thinking and having a powerful impact on my state of mind and peace of heart. *Don't give the Enemy a seat at your table* was quickly becoming more than a helpful quote. These nine words were becoming a weapon that was setting me free.

MOMENTUM GATHERS

A few weeks later, I was leading a morning Bible study for the coaches of a professional sports team. The team's season had been characterized by struggle and defeat, and the mood in the room felt low. Their critics were circling. I would guess there was a measure of internal suspicion and strife. I could see the angst and despair on their faces. The coaches were in a similar place to where I'd been the night I first texted my friend.

Midway through my message I felt a nudge from the Spirit to pivot my talk toward what God was teaching me through Psalm 23 and what I'd been learning about the table God prepares in the presence of our enemies. I described to them how I'd sent my friend a lengthy "woe is me, back me up" text and what he had replied to me.

When I uttered the phrase *Don't give the Enemy a seat at your table*, the atmosphere in the room shifted. The expression on many of the coaches' faces changed. Later I heard from several of them that those nine words landed just as powerfully for them as they had for me.

That same day I headed back to Passion for our scheduled all-team meeting. As I returned to Atlanta I called and asked for a table to be set up in the middle of the room with basic snacks and water glasses on it. I expanded on what I had shared that morning with the coaches and morphed the message into a visual experience, where I sat at a table with food on it and spoke on the promise of Psalm 23.

Again, the message landed with power. So much so that we fleshed it out into a full talk that I shared with our church the following Sunday. The food was a bit more sumptuous this time and the place settings a tad fancier. We had bountiful fruit and cheese plates. Cold cuts. Bread. Dessert.

Bam! Those nine words hit home again . . . deeply, profoundly. A mom of three who was in the midst of a contentious separation told me those words were exactly what she needed to hear. A college student wrestling with thoughts of suicide echoed her response. It was clear I wasn't the only one struggling, and the message wasn't just for me. It was meant to be shared with as many people as possible.

In time I had the privilege of sharing the message around the world, and the experience became refreshingly interactive for me as a communicator. I would start the message onstage but soon end up at the table, which had been situated beforehand in the midst of the people. At some point I'd pass food down the rows, encouraging people to enjoy a croissant or brownie or carrot stick and then pass the tray of food on to their neighbors. Delectable-looking desserts always got the biggest cheer.

But it wasn't about a potentially gimmicky illustration. The landslide of power was the realization that the King of the universe is inviting you and me to sit with Him at His table. Those nine words were memorable, but even more, they were packed with proven power. The story they conveyed was freeing and had instant application.

It's the story of a Good Shepherd who sees you and walks with you through the valley. It's about God setting a table of nourishment and refreshment in the midst of trouble. This message lets you see how you don't need to let the thoughts in your head run wild. These nine words are ultimately a message of victory.

TAKE BACK THE TABLE
PREPARED FOR YOU

That's why I've written this book. I want to help you see that you have power, through Jesus Christ, to take authority over who sits at your table—over who influences your thinking. You can take back your freedom and control your thoughts and emotions. You don't need to be trapped by fear, despair, or rage. Your mind doesn't have to be stressed. You don't need to wrestle anymore with harmful thoughts. You are invited to an intimate relationship with the Almighty. The table He's prepared for you is one of peace, clarity, and abundance. You don't have to give the Enemy a seat at your table.

To be clear, the nine words that arrived on my phone screen are what God used to set in motion the chain of events that led to this book. Yet the potential that waits for you in these pages is rooted in something far greater than a text message from a friend. The promise of this book is anchored in a message from your Creator. His words to you in Scripture are alive and powerful. His words can break the strongholds that have held you captive for years. They can help you think clearly again. His words will give you brand-new sight.

In the pages to come, we'll crack open Psalm 23 in a fresh way. And we'll particularly highlight verse 5: "You prepare a table before me in the presence of my enemies." I'll address the lies the Enemy feeds you as he weasels his way into a seat at the table that's intended for you and your King. I'll outline ways to defeat those lies and help you find victory, peace, and security in the midst of any challenging circumstance or situation. And I'll give you practical, helpful encouragement to stand firm in Jesus and take control of your thoughts and fears.

The Devil wants nothing more than to crush you. He wants to steal from you everything you value. He wants to kill everything in your life that's good. Ultimately, he wants to destroy you. If he can claim the victory over your mind, he can eventually claim the victory over your life.

But the message of Psalm 23 is that the Good Shepherd prepares a table for you. It's a table for two, and the Devil is not invited to sit. This book offers an all-encompassing message that can be applied to any number of hard situations. It will help you find encouragement, hope, and strength in the midst of your valley. You don't need to listen to the voices of fear, rage, lust, insecurity, anxiety, despair, temptation, or defeat.

I'm in this battle with you. I preach this same message to myself again and again, and I am confident that our Good Shepherd will be glorified as He leads us to win the fight for our minds. So let's go there together. Me and you. It's time to take back what the Enemy has stolen. Let's turn the page to take a closer look at what the Good Shepherd's table is all about.

THE TWENTY-THIRD PSALM—REMIX

Our good friends Jay and Katherine Wolf met years ago as freshmen at Samford University and soon fell in love. He was heading for a career in law. She was literally crowned Miss Samford—smart, beautiful, and confident.

In 2004, newly graduated, they married and vowed to love each other in sickness and health. They soon moved from Atlanta to Malibu, California, where Jay entered law school at Pepperdine University and Katherine pursued a career in acting and modeling. For a couple of years everything went smoothly. In 2007, they had their first child, a boy. All was going well.

One afternoon six months after Katherine had given birth,

she felt dizzy and sick to her stomach. Her hands, arms, and legs went numb. She walked into the living room to turn down the TV. She wobbled once, twice, and then suddenly collapsed. Jay was home and called 911. Katherine was rushed to the hospital and diagnosed with a massive brain stem stroke. She wasn't expected to live. To save her life, more than half of her cerebellum was removed. The surgery took more than sixteen hours. Katherine was twenty-six.

Miraculously, Katherine survived the sudden ordeal, yet the story of their "new normal" was only beginning. For two months, Katherine lay unconscious. For forty days she stayed in intensive care. She had to relearn how to talk and eat. It took eighteen months to walk again. Years of rehabilitation and recovery followed, along with ten more surgeries. Katherine's body would never fully heal from the stroke.

Today, Katherine lives with long-term limitations. She is partially deaf and can't swallow normally or see well. Part of her face shows the effects of paralysis. Her speech is slurred. Mostly she uses a wheelchair to get around. Yet Katherine and Jay exude a remarkable kind of faith. It's a faith deeply rooted in the confidence that there's purpose in pain. As a result, they are a huge force for the kingdom of God. Through their books and messages, they bring much hope to suffering people everywhere.[1]

Few of us have been through the depth of what Katherine and Jay have experienced. But all of us have experienced a life less than perfect. When it comes to not giving the Enemy a seat at your table, we have to start by wrapping our minds around this difficult truth: life is hard, yet Jesus invites us to follow Him anyway.

AN "EVEN THOUGH . . . I WILL" FAITH

On page after page in Scripture, we find people in situations where life has closed in on them. It might seem logical for them to chuck their faith. We wouldn't be surprised if they turned away from God in the midst of difficulty, or if they leaned toward their favorite addiction in an attempt to feel better. Unfortunately, that's what too many people do when the going gets tough.

See, when life turns hard for us, we're almost always tempted to welcome the Enemy at our table. But when we realize that Jesus invites us to follow Him *even though* life is hard, we discover the foundational truth for winning the battle for our minds.

This is the depth of faith we see throughout the Bible. Three Hebrew young men, Shadrach, Meshach, and Abednego, worshipped God in an era when King Nebuchadnezzar had commanded everybody to worship only a huge, gold statue of himself. The goal of Shadrach, Meshach, and Abednego was to be obedient to God's call on their lives. When the music played (the signal for everybody to fall down and worship the golden statue), Shadrach,

Meshach, and Abednego remained standing. Because of their righteous actions, they wound up being thrown into a raging fire. What was God thinking? Surely that made no sense. They didn't do anything wrong. Shouldn't they be rewarded for their righteous living? Wasn't God for them and not against them?

The faith of Shadrach, Meshach, and Abednego didn't deflate. Instead, their faith inflated. Even on the edge of a fiery furnace, they were able to say to the king, "If we are thrown into the blazing furnace, the God we serve is able to deliver us from it, and he will deliver us from Your Majesty's hand. But even if he does not, we want you to know, Your Majesty, that we will not serve your gods or worship the image of gold you have set up" (Daniel 3:17–18). Rescued out of their circumstances or left to go through the fire—either way—they would stay true to God.

Or take a look at Paul and Silas. They found themselves in prison. Their crime? They set free a female slave from demonic oppression. They did the right thing. Even then, the citizens of the city of Philippi gathered in a furious mob and dragged Paul and Silas before the authorities. They were severely beaten and thrown in jail. Paul and Silas were trying to honor God. They'd been on a mission trip, and this is what they got? Nobody would have faulted them if they had abandoned the faith, or whined and complained, or turned to some sort of an addiction in an attempt to quell their pain. But no. It was midnight. Their feet were fastened in stocks. Their backs were bloody and raw. And Paul and

Silas were praying and singing songs of praise (Acts 16:16–40). That's a faith that inflates during difficult times.

I look at Paul and Silas; at Shadrach, Meshach, and Abednego; and at all the people throughout Scripture who encountered times of intense trouble yet went bigger with their faith, and I marvel. The prophet Habakkuk stated it clearly when he cried out:

> Even though the fig trees have no fruit
>> and no grapes grow on the vines,
> even though the olive crop fails
>> and the fields produce no grain,
> even though the sheep all die
>> and the cattle stalls are empty,
> I will still be joyful and glad,
>> because the LORD God is my savior.
>
> (Habakkuk 3:17–18 GNT)

The last two lines indicate huge faith. And did you notice the two phrases repeated three times in Habakkuk's prayer?

Even though . . . I will . . .

Habakkuk basically said, "*Even though* there's no harvest, and *even though* crops fail, and *even though* the fields are desolate, and *even though* the stalls of provision are empty, *I will* still be joyful and glad because the Lord God is my Savior. I have not lost my faith. In fact, my faith is even greater. I'm still going to rejoice in the Lord. I'm still going to worship God. I'm not going to get sidetracked by attitudes or actions that harm me. When I encounter hard times, my faith inflates."

Those two phrases lay out a powerful cause-and-effect relationship as an example for us to follow. *Even though* bad things happen, *I will* still praise the Lord. *Even though* bad things happen, *I will* not let my mind be lost to the Enemy.

That's the kind of faith I see in Jay and Katherine Wolf. As I wrote this chapter, they received word that new tests were needed to clarify a previously undetected set of neurological challenges. Depending on the results of those tests, they could be facing more challenging headwinds. They asked Shelley and me to pray for them before the scans were performed. When we finished praying, Katherine prayed for us about a storm that Shelley and I were navigating. In Katherine's prayer, she quoted Habakkuk 3:17–18. We said our amens, and I told her I was just about to write those exact verses.

She said, "I love the last verse: 'GOD the Lord is my strength; He makes my feet like those of a deer; He makes me walk upon the heights!' I clung to those words when I was learning to walk again" (v. 19 BSB). Back in 2009, having received less-than-optimistic diagnoses from doctors, she personalized the passage for her situation:

> Though I cannot walk,
> And I am confined to a wheelchair;

> Though half my face is paralyzed,
> And I cannot even smile;
> Though I am extremely impaired,
> And I cannot take care of my baby;
> Yet I will rejoice in the Lord,
> I will be joyful in God my Savior!

This is not the faith of a Christian who believes in God only when the sun shines. This is not a faith that wilts under pressure. This faith flourishes even though the pressure is on. This faith says, *Even though bad things are happening, I will praise the Lord.*

How might you personalize Habakkuk's prayer?

> Even though I am under intense financial pressure . . .
> Even though my spouse is with another person right now . . .
> Even though we are in a global crisis . . .
> Even though _____ . . .
> Yet I will rejoice in the Lord.
> I will be joyful in God my Savior!

Developing this kind of "even though / I will" faith changes the temperature and trajectory of your life. When the pressure mounts, this kind of faith doesn't deflate. Instead, it actually inflates. It becomes bolder. More resolute and undaunted. More robust.

The development of an "even though" kind of faith has a lot to do with where we position our focus. We can develop this kind of faith, in Jesus' name, and the development of this faith is the foundational principle behind not giving the Enemy a seat at our table. To do that, we need to root our thinking in a well-known but widely untapped biblical promise.

AN ANCIENT SONG BRINGS NEW STRENGTH

If I asked you what the most well-known passage of Scripture is, maybe you'd say John 3:16. Sure, you've seen it scrawled on signs and held up at sporting events. But I think Psalm 23 might be even more famous. You hear this passage recited at weddings and funerals. It's been preached about, painted about, and sculpted. It's on memes scattered across social media. You'll find snippets of it in movies such as *Pale Rider* and *Titanic*. It's found in any number of songs—classics by Bach and Schubert, countless hymns and worship songs, and even Coolio's "Gangsta's Paradise."

Psalm 23 is woven into the very fabric of our culture, yet if your church background is similar to mine, we both need to clear away the cobwebs. Because when I say Psalm 23, it's too easy to rattle off those famous words without even thinking.

The Lord is my shepherd, I shall not want . . . No problem there. *Green pastures. Quiet waters. The valley of the shadow. The rod. The staff. The table. The oily head.* Sure, I know what you're talking about.

We need to erase any tame and churchy thoughts about this psalm because it's highly relevant to what we're experiencing in our culture today. Right here, right now. We need to ask God to help us throw away the imagery of Grandma's needlepoint bookmark with the shepherd's crook and help us see how this passage packs an unbelievably powerful promise for us.

This passage depicts God as a personal and attentive Shepherd, One who intimately cares for the sheep yet is tough enough to defend them against attacks. This Shepherd will make sure you are rested and well fed. But He'll also beat back all those who threaten your safety and well-being. In time, we see this Shepherd most clearly in the person of Jesus Christ.

In John 10:1–21 Jesus outlined how He Himself is the Good Shepherd. Jesus knows His sheep—us. He protects us from thieves and robbers. He laid down His life for us. He guides us, and we are able to listen for His voice and know His voice. John 10 personifies Jesus as the Good Shepherd of Psalm 23. And in Psalm 23, the attributes and actions of the Shepherd-God are true of the Shepherd-Jesus. We know this because Hebrews 13:8 states plainly that "Jesus Christ is the same yesterday and today and forever." Here's the incredible invitation: Jesus is saying, *I want to be your Good Shepherd.* He is a personal, involved God who wants to shepherd your life. Can we just stop and breathe in this reality? The Good Shepherd, who also happens to be God, is offering to lead you through every moment of your life!

The key for us, then, is that we allow Jesus to shepherd us. See, all of us are shepherded whether we realize it or not. Your shepherd might not be Jesus. But something is going to lead you. Second Peter 2:19 says, "People are slaves to whatever has mastered them." So maybe the culture is going to lead you. The anthem of the world is going to lead you. You're going to go with whatever the social media flow is, and that's going to lead you.

Some of you are saying, *Nah, I don't have a shepherd. Nobody leads me. I call the shots. I make all the decisions around here.* Great—then you are your own shepherd. You're leading yourself. You're depending on yourself to guide you to still water and green pastures. One thing is for sure: if you are your own shepherd, it is likely you *are* in want. Unfortunately, when people take the reins of their own lives, they end up paraphrasing Psalm 23 into something like this:

> I am my own shepherd,
> and I'm a mess.

I don't have everything I need. That's for sure.

I wouldn't know still water if it were staring right at me.

I haven't taken a rest in a green pasture for quite a
while now.

I don't walk along paths of righteousness, but I know what
fear and evil are.

I seek comfort wherever I can get it.

I can't stand my enemies. I want to hurt them.

My cup definitely overflows—I'm full of angst, consumed
by anger and sorrow and rage. I'm so full I easily spill
over. I'm packed so tight, it doesn't take much for me
to explode.

I don't know what's going to follow me all the days of my
life, but I can tell you this one thing:

My soul? Not so great.

When you allow Jesus to be your Shepherd, He steps into this stressed-out culture and becomes your replenishing guide. He leads you, watches over you, and gives you rest. Jesus gives you purpose. He shows you how to deal with your enemies so they don't tear you apart inside. Jesus gives you a hope and a future, and He'll restore your soul. He'll give you goodness and love for today, for tomorrow, and for every day for the rest of your life. Jesus will even give you an eternity with Him in paradise.

All of that is found in the promises of Psalm 23. If you haven't allowed Jesus to lead your life, why not do so right now? If you let Him lead you, you're not going to lack a thing. And your life will change for the better.

But there's something else: when you allow Jesus to lead you, it's not simply about Him giving you good things or doing helpful things for you. In Psalm 23 we see the first way the Good Shepherd is going to lead you will require Him making you do something.

WHY IT'S GOOD TO BE LED

No way, you're saying. *I'm getting off the bus right here. We're not even two chapters into this book yet, and already Jesus is going to make me do something?*

Hold on. This mandate is foundational to how Jesus cares for you. He loves you enough to make you do something vital that you are not inclined to know how to do (or choose to do) on your own. But you're going to like it—because He makes you lie down in green pastures.

Sure, you can lie down on rocky ground if you want to. You can lie down in the heat and the dust. But Jesus says, *Lie down in green pastures. Get some rest. Stop trying to manage all the outcomes. Take a break in the midst of the craziness of your day and acknowledge that I'm a Good Shepherd and I have your best interest at heart. By the way, while you're resting, go ahead and eat some green grass. Allow Me to nourish your soul. That's how I operate. I love you and take care of you, and any directive that I give you will be for your own benefit.*

See, when God refers to us as sheep, it's a reflection of how we are wired, although it's not necessarily a compliment. Sheep need leadership. God's not saying that we're cute and cuddly. He's saying it's far too easy for us to have the wool pulled over our eyes. We don't see with as much discernment as we should. We don't even rest when we need to. When it comes to making decisions about our well-being, we're not always überintellects.

Any guesses why the water that the Good Shepherd leads His sheep to is specifically described as "still"? It's because sheep lack self-awareness. If a sheep sees a roaring river, it thinks that's a good place to get its thirst quenched. Never mind that sheep are covered with five sweaters' worth of wool. The sheep gets so jazzed at the sight of any water that he sticks his head straight down into that rushing river. All fifteen pounds of wool become soaking wet. *Kersplash.* The sheep gets sucked straight into the roaring river. Now he's heading for the rapids, looking back for a bailout from the shepherd . . . *baaaa!*

Fortunately, the Good Shepherd carries a crook—a long, sturdy stick with a hook at one end. Whenever we start heading toward things that initially look good but ultimately lead to our destruction, Jesus pulls us back to safety. Provided, of course, we let Him lead. God doesn't force us to follow Him. Sometimes only our noses become wet in the rushing water and Jesus catches us quickly. Sometimes we fight the Shepherd's crook and dive straight into the river. We're in the rapids now, heavy, soaked, and waterlogged, getting dragged under by the weight of our foolish choices. We've thumbed our sheep-noses for so long at the Shepherd that the river is washing us away to our destruction. We're headed out to sea.

I know I need a Good Shepherd. I've been a Christian for many years, yet I'm keenly aware of my need to constantly surrender the leadership of my life to God. I'm far too prone to stick my head into any rushing stream that looks good. I'm not as adept at making intelligent decisions as I think I am. I don't naturally lie down in green pastures, so I welcome this command. I need the Good Shepherd to be near, and I need to listen for His voice when He says, *No, Louie, we're not drinking there. We're not going up to the edge of Niagara Falls looking for our thirst to be quenched. Come over to this quiet little pool instead. Drink up at the quiet waters—and live.*

Leading us to still water is a foundational activity of a shepherd, and as such, it's essential to what I want to talk about in this book—you winning the battle of your mind. That's why I mention it in this early chapter. In a word, the Good Shepherd is . . . *good*. Because of His great love for us, Jesus always acts with our ultimate well-being in mind. The goodness of God can be found in all He is and says and does.

Yet the emphasis of the mid-to-later portions of Psalm 23 is what I want us to focus on because these verses point us to the "even though" type of faith I've mentioned. When we develop this kind of faith, it helps change our lives for good. In Psalm 23:4 we find these words, and they set up the context of the verses to come: "*Even though* I walk through the darkest valley, *I will* fear no evil."

Did you see the "even though / I will" in that famous verse? It's amazing that the Good Shepherd walks with us right through the valley of the shadow of death. God is there with us through real hardship. He's with us when a loved one gets sick. He's with us when we bury someone we care for. He's close when our heart is shattered. He's close when we lose some sort of good thing we'd hoped for. Maybe you're experiencing the death of a relationship or the loss of a dream. You tried to get into a certain program, but it didn't work out. You were heading for a certain job but didn't get it. You were positive a certain person was interested in you, but it turned out that person wanted to be only friends. Maybe you and your spouse were trying to conceive a child, but that window closed.

We can experience any number of losses in the valley of the shadow of death. Loss is a part of our story as humans. We all walk through grief, disappointment, and discouragement. That's why it's so key that *even though* King David walked through such great difficulty, he declared, "*I will* fear no evil." The Good Shepherd was there to guide and comfort him. Just as we did with Habakkuk's prayer, we can make this psalm personal in our lives.

How can you honestly say you're not afraid? The answer is shown in the second part of verse 4. We won't solve all the problems around us. We don't avoid every difficulty that comes our way. Yet we don't need to fear any evil, because the Good Shepherd is with us. His rod and staff comfort us. Let's not rush by this truth. Look at it slowly. Carefully.

God Almighty *is with us.*

No matter the troubles you're walking through right now, the good news is not simply that God will help you. That's not the whole message. The message is that God *is with you.* He's with you in the sickness. He's with you at the grave. He's with you when the job opportunity doesn't come through. He's with you when you receive hard news. He's with you in the chemo ward. He's with you in the storm, and in the wind, and in the trial, and in the valley. God Almighty—your Good Shepherd—is right there in the midst of the difficulty with you. This is a game-changing revelation, and it shifts your prayer life. Because you don't need to pray anymore, *God, I'm in a storm—help me.* Instead, you pray, *God, I'm in a storm. Thank You for being in this storm with me. You've got my back. How are we going to get through this together?*

Peace and victory and freedom don't come from sitting around wishing we didn't have any problems or pain. No, the

GOD ALMIGHTY—
YOUR GOOD
SHEPHERD—
IS RIGHT
THERE IN THE
MIDST OF THE
DIFFICULTY
WITH YOU.

―――――――――

reality is that we all will be led through the valley of the shadow of death in some way, shape, or form. Jesus promises in Psalm 23 that peace, victory, and freedom will come *in the midst of* problems, pain, and loss. That's how we develop an "even though" kind of faith. We live by knowing that, in the midst of a broken world, God Almighty is with us.

A TABLE IN THE CONFLICT

Verse 5 of Psalm 23 is one of the most powerful verses in all of Scripture, and we're going to dwell on this verse in expanding circles for much of the rest of this book, so I wanted you to see some of the truths that led to this point in the psalm first. A beautiful twist is found in this verse. Remember how it says that *God prepares a table before us in the presence of our enemies*?

I'm sure if I'd written that verse, I would have written it differently. If God is going to prepare a table for me, well, that's awesome. But I think it should be a table for me in *God's presence*. Not the presence of my enemies. Hey, come on, God—if I were writing this, I'd have You reserve a table by the window so while we eat together I can watch You smoke my enemies! Get them out of here. I don't want the enemies anywhere near me when I eat a meal—much less have dessert.

But that's not how Psalm 23:5 was written. God has prepared a table right in the middle of the battle. That table is laden with the richest of fare—and it's all good food for us to eat—yet that table is set right in the midst of the chemo ward. God has set out the silverware, and He's invited us to come and dine with Him—yet that table is right in the middle of our family being pulled apart. That table is right in the middle of job stress. It's smack-dab in the middle of relational tension. It's directly at the center of the hardships and arguments, the misunderstandings and persecutions, the depression and the death. Whatever we are battling, internally or externally, the table is right there in the middle of the trouble, at the epicenter of conflict.

Can you picture that table right now?

Sometimes the Bible uses the term *table* as a figurative expression for God's salvation, peace, and presence. Every Jewish listener would immediately know the significance of being invited to sit at someone's table, especially the table of the Lord. In days of old, before Jesus was incarnate and personally knowable as Savior and Friend, God's presence was represented in various ways. A cloud. Fire. Smoke that filled the room. As the story of God's people unfolded, God gave instructions for a tabernacle to be built. This was a place where sinful man could meet with holy God. One of the items to be placed in the tabernacle was a *table*, and on that table was to be placed the bread of the Presence. "Put the bread of the Presence on this table to be before me at all times" (Exodus 25:30).

Today, the same holy God invites us to dine with Him,

and the invitation comes at a high price: Jesus. Redemption is completed when rebels are now in fellowship with God, enjoying God's feast. Notice Isaiah 25:6, where "the LORD Almighty will prepare a feast of rich food for all peoples." Or Luke 13:29, where "people will . . . take their places at the feast in the kingdom of God."

All are welcome at the table of God's salvation. But the table described in Psalm 23:5 is a table of fellowship. It's a table meant for only you and the Good Shepherd. Don't worry; it's not exclusive in the sense that only one person is ever invited to this table. Rather, it's exclusive in the sense that everybody who is led by the Good Shepherd is invited to dine at this table with God. The Enemy is not welcome to sit here. If you are following Christ, then God has prepared such a table for you.

Okay, so let's picture this table together. Two seats are placed across from each other. The Good Shepherd stands on one side of the table. You stand on the other. Before you both sit, you first take in the feast that's set before your eyes. The specifics of your table will look different from mine. It's the Lord's table, to be clear, but He is setting the table with you in mind. On the table are all the foods you love to eat. Good food. Healthy food. Bountiful food. More than enough. You don't have to eat it all—it's not an invitation to gluttony. It's a true feast that satisfies your deepest longings. On the table is the kind of meal that makes you feel full and free at the same time.

Maybe the tray closest to you is laden with fresh fruit. A starter course. You see sun-warmed strawberries. Seedless watermelon. Ripened grapes. Crisp apples.

Another tray offers salads. There's crunchy romaine lettuce topped with extra-virgin olive oil, finely grated parmesan cheese, kosher salt, and freshly ground black pepper. Crunchy croutons are cut from hearty bread. Don't like a Caesar? How about a house salad, topped with fresh tomatoes and cucumbers? Off to the side is an epic charcuterie sampler.

A heavenly aroma wafts upward and catches your nose. Upon another tray sits the main course. For you meat eaters, it's grilled steak—golden brown and slightly charred on the outside, medium-rare and inviting on the inside. Or freshly caught brook trout, if you'd prefer. For vegetarians, it's orecchiette pasta with broccoli sauce. Or roasted chiles rellenos. Or delicious black bean enchiladas. Piping hot. Beautifully garnished.

Did I mention dessert? On the table is a delectable New York cheesecake. Hot apple pie with the smoothest, creamiest ice cream. Red velvet cake. Gooey brownies. Glazed donuts. Coconut cream pie.

Ready to eat?

You're a moment away from diving in, but suddenly—while you and the Good Shepherd are still standing behind your chairs—you notice you're not alone. Nobody is at the table except you and the Good Shepherd, but encircling you is a throng of people. You see them now. They're part of what makes this table so unique, because your enemies are still in view. The folks surrounding the table aren't happy you're here. They're scowling. Calling you names. Criticizing you, saying things about you that aren't true. They're out to undermine your efforts. They're filled with hate. Some want to stab you in the back.

The folks encircling you are representative of your troubles. Your problems. Your stressors. You're surrounded by calamity, pressure, anxiety, addiction, divorce, depression, family collapse, all sorts of pain. And then the unthinkable happens. Right in the middle of all the calamity and strife, the God of heaven calls you by name and says, "Please, sit down."

At this point you'd think it would be obvious that you would take the Good Shepherd up on His offer. But in today's fast-paced life, you and I can't be sure. It's more likely that we might stage a great social media photo, one that requires us to stand on our chairs to get just the right angle, and quickly post it to our feeds with the caption "Unreal meal today with my King." We only have time to snap the pic as we grab a to-go cup of coffee and dash off to our next appointment. "Thank You so much, Jesus! You are the best, man. I love You for it. This is all too much, really! I've got to jet to a meeting, but I'll definitely catch You later. For sure."

Or things could go quite differently. You and the Good Shepherd could both sit down.

"Are you thirsty?" He asks as He fills your glass with the freshest water.

Stunned and amazed, you try to process what is happening. *Is the God of the universe actually pouring me a glass of water?* You bite into a strawberry. You ladle up some hot buttered mashed potatoes. You sink your teeth into the juiciest of steaks.

This is the picture of "even though / I will" faith. *Even though I am surrounded by enemies, God has prepared a table for me, and I will sit down with Him.*

God's not chintzy. He doesn't have a scarcity mentality. He has a generosity mentality, and everything tastes as wonderful as it looks. You eat and you eat and you eat, and it's a wonderful meal. It's an experience that happens continually, moment by moment, for the rest of your life. This meal is at the core of your intimate relationship with God Almighty. He doesn't promise to eliminate the conflict. He hasn't removed you from the reality of trouble. But He has promised to prepare a table for you in the presence of your enemies.

Keep in mind, also, that in spite of all the delicious food you're diving into, the true importance of this table is not what's on it. The wonder of this meal is not the food.

It's about who you're at the table with.

A MEAL WITH ALMIGHTY GOD

We will talk in the pages that follow about the life-changing benefits that come as we recognize and embrace all that God is providing for us at His table. Benefits that are real and important, such as victory over sin and an unmuddied mind; freedom from bondage and the ability to take control of our fears. Yet it's important to see from the start that the ultimate benefit for us all is not something God gives us. It's God Himself. That's the powerful message at the heart of this book. God is sitting at the table with us. God is walking with us through the valley of the shadow of death. We are invited to have a relationship with Almighty God.

This is not a self-help book where I'm giving you three steps to a pain-free life. It's a book of worship, where we see Jesus in new and biblical ways, and then respond in awe to Jesus the Great King. We see our identity rooted and established in Jesus, and our lives change because the Good Shepherd leads us every step of the way.

How easy it is for us to forget—or never fully know—who our dinner companion truly is. Do you know who's at the table with you? Let's just linger over this a minute so we catch its weight, because in 1 Timothy 1:17, God is described as "the King of the ages, immortal, invisible, the only God" (ESV).

That's who's at the table with you.

The apostle Paul, in Romans 11:33 and 36, described your dinner companion this way: "Oh, the depth of the riches and wisdom and knowledge of God! How unsearchable are his judgments and how inscrutable his ways! . . . For from him and through him and to him are all things. To him be glory forever. Amen" (ESV).

That's who's at the table with you.

The ancient spiritual leader Job described your dinner companion in comparison to the vastness of space, how earth is suspended as if over nothing, how God wraps up waters in His cloud and can cover the face of the full moon. God marks out the horizon and causes the pillars of heaven to quake; He can churn up the sea or blow upon the skies so they become fair. "And these are but the outer fringe of his works," Job said. "How faint the whisper we hear of him! Who then can understand the thunder of his power?" (Job 26:14).

That's who sits at your table with you.

Your real reward is being at dinner with Jesus. The wonder and power of Psalm 23:5 is that it's not simply a nice passage of Scripture to embroider and stick on a wall. Seated at your table is God Almighty!

Okay. The meal's going great. It's just you and Jesus. You're feasting with Him and enjoying an unencumbered relationship together. You know that across the table is the Great King, and that He and He alone is your true and best reward. You know He loves you. But as I mentioned earlier, someone else—your greatest Enemy—wants in and is working persistently, stealthily, to sit at this table with you. That person is definitely not invited, but he knows that if he can win the battle of your mind, he can destroy you.

THREE

MIND IF I SIT DOWN?

I can still feel the sweat accumulating on my palms.[1]

It was my wife Shelley's birthday, and I had planned a special dinner at one of her favorite restaurants. Just the two of us. Shelley had really been looking forward to this night out, so I wanted to do everything I could to make it special for her.

There we were at our perfect dinner. Amazing city. Killer vibe. Exceptional food. Just us, though we were seated at a table for four. Midway through what was an absolutely stellar meal, a young man I hadn't met before walked by on his way out of the restaurant and did a double take. "Louie Giglio?" he said, shocked. "Is that you? No way, I can't believe I'm seeing you here. Two months ago I was at a conference you spoke at, and God really impacted my life!"

I looked up and said, "Nice to meet you. And really cool to hear that God spoke to you in such a powerful way. Thanks for saying hello."

"Nice to meet you too," he said as he continued toward the door.

Shelley and I picked back up with our conversation and continued to enjoy our dinner. A few minutes passed, and I noticed the same young man come back into the restaurant and head straight for our table. I quickly scanned the table for sunglasses, keys, a wallet. He must have accidently left something behind when he stopped to say hi.

"Hey, I hope this doesn't sound weird," he said when he reached our table, "but when I got outside and told my friend I'd seen you as we were leaving, she said, 'You've got to go back and talk to him.' See, I've been wanting to share something with you that God has laid on my heart ever since that conference. And, crazy, here you are. I never thought I'd see you. Mind if I sit down?" Without waiting for a reply, he reached for one of the empty chairs at our table.

"Hey, I'd love to hear what God has done in your life," I said quickly. "But can we find another time to connect? It's my wife's birthday, and we're having a special night out. Let's touch base another time, okay?"

The guy looked at Shelley and said curtly, "Happy birthday."

Then he immediately turned his attention back to me and started to sit down in the chair.

What?!

Does anybody get what had just happened? My options weren't great at that point. That's when my palms turned sweaty. Tension filled my gut. On one hand, I could invite this stranger to my wife's special birthday dinner. Just the three of us. On the other hand, I was worried that what I was about to say to him next was going to make me sound insensitive.

The point of this story isn't what went down at that restaurant with that guy (a supernice, well-meaning guy, no doubt) or how Shelley and I tried to disentangle ourselves from an awkward moment. The point is for all of us to take a hard look at the velocity of the moment. It only took a millisecond for that guy to pull up a seat at our table, and the same can be true for how fast the Enemy can sit down at your table. In less time than it takes to snap your fingers—if you're not careful—the Enemy can pull up a seat at the table your Shepherd has prepared for you. Suddenly, it's not just you and God Almighty at your table anymore.

Now it's you and God and the Devil.

The Enemy only needs the tiniest crack. A sliver of opportunity. The smallest window of doubt or uncertainty. Just like that, the Devil is sitting at *your* table, beginning to win the battle for your mind.

IN LESS TIME THAN
IT TAKES TO SNAP
YOUR FINGERS—
IF YOU'RE NOT
CAREFUL—THE
ENEMY CAN
PULL UP A SEAT
AT THE TABLE
YOUR SHEPHERD
HAS PREPARED
FOR YOU.

———————————————

TAKING BACK OUR FREEDOM

We've come to accept the Enemy sitting at our table as normal. That's a big problem. We give him permission anytime we say things like, "Oh, that's just the way it is these days. Anxiety is just part of the equation. We're all anxious, and there's nothing we can do about it. Life's just so chaotic today. Of course we're all strangled by worry. Look at any news feed. Why wouldn't I be afraid?"

In the same way, we accept the false narrative about our lives that *we aren't worth much to God . . .* or anybody else, for that matter. We think people don't get us. Or they don't value us. Or they are flat-out against us.

Or we flip to the other point of view. We think we deserve more, so we allow envy and greed and comparison to cannibalize our God-given identity. We scroll our way through social media feeds determined to get what other people have—or, better yet, to get more.

More stuff. That's what we need. More friends. More layers of protection. More likes. Or maybe another table. After all, we all live in a corrupted culture, and we know it. Why stress over a little lust here, or a moment or two of pleasure there? Before you know it, you talk like the Devil and think the thoughts he wants you to dwell on.

That's just the way it is, right?

No! Allowing the Enemy to have a say in our lives should not be normal. In Jesus' name, we can refuse him and all his ways. We don't need to accept them. He leads us to sins that are harming us and choking the life out of this generation, but they don't have to stay in our lives. Romans 8:10–12 says that the same Holy Spirit who raised Jesus from the dead lives inside of us. This same resurrection power is available to us. Jesus Christ has broken the power of sin, and God's invitation to us is to embrace a new mindset and a new way of living. In Jesus' name we are to think of ourselves as dead to the power of sin. In Jesus' name we don't have to let the voice of the Enemy control the way we live. In Jesus' name we don't have to give in to sinful desires; we can win the battle for our minds. Thanks to Jesus, we are no longer slaves. We are set free. We are alive. We are children of God.

See, we create a big problem when we grasp only the first part of Psalm 23:4 (walking through the valley) but opt out of remembering what comes next (God's promise to be with us in the midst of difficulties). Whenever we camp in the valley and stay there, focused on the difficulties in our lives, we are prompted by the Enemy to go another direction. We experience trials or hardships or persecution or loneliness, and we think, *Well, I'm in the valley of the shadow now. God didn't come through for me. I prayed for such and such, and God didn't answer that prayer the way I wanted, so I'm going to stay in the valley. I was obedient to God, but God didn't reward me as I hoped. So I'm going to turn to sin in an effort to feel better.*

Did you hear that? That's the sound of a chair quickly being dragged across the floor. It's still a table for two, but now an unwelcome visitor has shown up.

YOUR SWIFT AND VICIOUS ENEMY

When this unwelcome visitor shows up, he's often quiet at first. Friendly even. You might not recognize him when he first sits down. The Devil doesn't arrive with a brightly flashing neon pitchfork. He doesn't sit down with a growl and threaten to gouge out your eyes. No. At first, it's simply another person seated next to you, helping himself to your brownie, wondering aloud which water glass is his, inadvertently wiping his mouth with your napkin.

It takes only a second. The unwelcome visitor sits down so swiftly and casually it's hard to discern his true character. He often appears to be on your side at the start. He promises you relief from your troubles. Second Corinthians 11:14 describes how Satan "masquerades as an angel of light," which means that the Devil rarely comes to the table showing his true colors—someone whose sole purpose is to "steal and kill and destroy" (John 10:10). Instead, the Devil takes the form of someone who's helpful, someone who appears to have your best interest at heart, someone who offers you respite from whatever pain you're feeling.

Hey, how's it going? he might ask. *You doing okay? You don't look so good. How's everything at work? I don't honestly know how you do it! Your boss is such a jerk. I mean really, you're a real trooper to hang in there and put up with that idiot! So, how are things at home? Still rough? Man, I pity you. I really do. Mind if I have another cupcake? These things are delicious!*

He might even quote Scripture to you. The Devil did that when he tempted Jesus (Matthew 4; Luke 4). Basically, the Devil said to Jesus, *Here, check out this one verse taken out of context— it's the big answer to what You're going through. Here, this one verse will be just the ticket You need.*

Your Enemy will use whatever devices are available to worm his thoughts inside your brain. Maybe it's a movie you watch, a series of subtly influential memes that flash by on social media, or a conversation between two people that happens within earshot. You're not positive how the Devil's thoughts got in your mind, but they're certainly in there now. He'll kick you when you're down. Maybe you're lonely. Or angry. Or tired. Whenever you feel burdened or pressured, you become more susceptible to evil's influence. First John 2:16 describes how three big items in the Devil's tool kit are "the lust of the flesh, the lust of the eyes, and the pride of life." That means the Devil can take anything the body naturally desires and use it to harm us—that's the lust of the flesh at work. The Devil can use anything we see and wish for as part of his trap to lead us toward destruction—that's the lust of the eyes. The pride of life, in this case, is a harmful sort of bragging or boasting or showmanship or ambition that causes us to have too much confidence in ourselves. The Devil will use that too.

Often the Devil appears empathetic. That's how he worked on Eve way back in the garden of Eden. Genesis 3 describes how the Devil, in the form of a serpent, prompted Eve to question if God was truly good. The Devil showed Eve the forbidden fruit and pointed out how beautiful it was. *Surely God is withholding something from you, something you truly need*, the Enemy whispered. Soon Eve was agreeing with the Devil, nodding her head, motioning to Adam, bent on convincing her husband and herself that the fruit was indeed "good for food and pleasing to the eye, and also desirable for gaining wisdom" (v. 6).

In whatever way the Devil gains access to your table, his goals are always the same. He wants to gain access to your mind so he can destroy you. He wants to get inside your head so harmful thoughts can be planted within you. Those thoughts will grow unchecked and spill out into actions. He wants you to be overtaken by wickedness. He wants to steal everything that is valuable from you. He wants to kill your relationship with God. He wants to cause division between you and the people who care for you. The Devil is not gentle—not in the long run. He was "a murderer from the beginning" (John 8:44), and he sets snares that capture people so they do his will (2 Timothy 2:26). The Devil is vicious and cruel, and he's always prowling around "like a roaring lion looking for someone to devour" (1 Peter 5:8).

That *someone* is you.

HAS THE ENEMY TAKEN A SEAT?

With all his trickery, it can be hard to recognize the Enemy's voice. He was prowling around Eve in the garden of Eden. He was prowling around the night Jesus was betrayed. It's not up to us to stop his prowling. But it is up to us to keep him from sitting at our table.

Rest assured: you have the power as a son or daughter of Jesus Christ to exercise faith that's defiant of the Devil's whisper. You can say, "In Jesus' name, I won't entertain your words, your thoughts, your influence."

What if the Devil is already sitting at your table and you haven't even recognized that he's there? Is it possible you've become so accustomed to the negative thoughts and destructive emotions that you don't even realize the Enemy is eating your lunch?

How do you know if the Enemy is already sitting at your table? By the predominant, relentless fiery arrows that are flying most furiously from the Devil's arsenal of weapons. We first need to recognize those lies and acknowledge their destructive powers in our lives before we unfold how they can be extinguished in Jesus' name.

FOUR

DEADLY LIES EXPOSED

I grew up in a big church in downtown Atlanta. When I was twelve, I remember being in our seventh-grade boys' Sunday school room. Tan linoleum floor. Cinderblock walls, also tan. Metal folding chairs. Maps of Paul's missionary journeys on the wall. A window with blinds—always closed. And on the far wall a big painting of the "meek and mild" Jesus. You know what I'm talking about? His face was pale. He looked like He hadn't been outside in a long time. His robe was perfect. His hair was perfect. He had a wooly lamb on His shoulders and a crook in His hand—and Jesus was gazing off into Foreverland with a faraway look in His eyes. But Olan Mills Portrait Studios Jesus is nothing like the real thing.

He's your hero. Your defender. He's the mighty Son of God!

When you are up against life and death, when your back's against the wall, when circumstances are poised to take you out, and when the Devil is whispering lies in your ear, you need to know there's an all-powerful Good Shepherd with a rod in one hand and a staff in the other. That's the Jesus of Psalm 23. That's why we find comfort in His presence. With that staff, the Good Shepherd can grab you and pull you to safety. And with that rod, He can crush any prowling lion or raging bear that charges toward you.

King David, who wrote Psalm 23, had taken on a lion and a bear and pounded them into the ground (1 Samuel 17:34–36). David understood what God said when He promised to be with us through the valley of the shadow of death. Jesus is there in the midst of the pressure with us, and He's not just standing around with His hands in His pockets. He's there to rescue us when necessary, to protect us at all costs, and to fill our cups to overflowing. We don't need to watch over our shoulders anymore. God prepares a table for us in the midst of our enemies. Jesus is watching them, guarding us, so we can keep our attention fully fixed on the face of the Good Shepherd—Jesus, our Savior.

Yet, as mentioned, it's strategic to be able to spot the enemy's lies—not so you can focus on the lies but so you can avoid them and fix your gaze back toward the Good Shepherd. When you are able to spot the following lies that are coming your direction, you can overcome them and win the battle for your mind with truth in Jesus' name.

THE LIE OF COMPARISON

First, if you've heard recently that it's better at another table, then you can be certain the Enemy is at *your* table. Jesus' table, the one He prepares for you, is about life and life abundantly (John 10:10). Any table other than God's table is about stealing, killing, and destroying. When the Devil sits at your table, he often points to another table and talks about how amazing it is somewhere else. He points to a place that's not the table where God is and says, *That, over there. That's the solution to your problem.*

See, the Devil is the worst kind of salesman. He tells you exactly what you want to hear and shows you exactly what you think you're looking for. He doesn't come to the table and announce to you that he's going to kill you. He comes to the table with an offer to seduce you. But ultimately, he's not selling you truth. He's not selling you life. No. He's selling you lies. He's selling you death.

Woven into the Devil's pitch that it's better at another table is the trickery of comparison. The Devil always tells you that there's a better table somewhere else. *Surely you should leave your spouse and hook up with someone else. Life will be better there, right? That's the solution to all your problems. If you could just be with somebody else. Surely you should run with that other crowd, the crowd that's not sitting at the table with Almighty God. If you could just abandon all you know to be true and go do your own thing for a season, that's going to be what you want. Surely at another table—a table without fellowship with God—there's more life, more food, more satisfaction, more joy, more of what you're looking for.*

Don't give in to that lie. The Devil loves for you to look at your life and compare it with somebody else's so you wish you had what they had. He'll mix in a little jealousy and sift in a little coveting and add a dash of *woe is me* and throw in a few lines about how God must love that person more than you. Or about how God is blessing that person more than He's blessing you. Or about how surely God has withheld something you need. Pretty soon the Devil has you convinced that God isn't good. God hasn't blessed you. God doesn't love you. You missed out on something good because God is mean or God forgot about you or God's been lying to you all this time.

We call this "the grass is always greener" syndrome. If you're not firmly seated at the table with the Almighty, if your eyes are not locked on those of the Good Shepherd, then you're distracted by the tyranny of comparison. Scanning the horizon around you, what do you see?

- Bob has a better position in the company. Cutting a few corners has worked out for him. That's why he's driving the new ride and you're struggling to buy your teenager a decent car. That's why he and his wife just added that fancy pool at their house with the rock waterfall in their backyard.

- Or look at Jasmine. Every post on her accounts is perfect. Her kids. Their vacation. Her little She Shed her husband, Ronnie, built behind their house.

- Curt, the guy you met at the gym, finally ditched his wife and dysfunctional family and got detangled from his crazy mother-in-law and is living in Sonoma with a new chick. He seems so carefree and happy.

- Anita quit the church (and her entry-level job at the wireless phone company) and is doing the RV thing in Utah. No responsibilities. No commitments. No baggage.

The Enemy masterfully paints an inviting picture of freedom. It's over there—where the grass is always greener. These thoughts that you can shirk commitments and have it your way don't come from Jesus. He comes to give life and give it to the full.

Are you moving away from what you know is right and good as you're reading these words? Are you thinking about bailing on what you've committed to? Are you close to doing something that you know is contrary to God's best? Something you know you'll regret? Or have you already made the jump away from Jesus, and you're quickly discovering that the "greener grass" is less than you bargained for? If so, the Enemy is at your table.

But you don't have to live this way. Jesus is calling you back to His table, to your table for two. Don't give the Enemy a seat at your table.

THE LIE THAT YOU'RE DOOMED

Second, if you've bought the lie that you're not going to make it, the Enemy is at your table. This voice tells you that life is hopeless. There's no way out. May as well just chuck it all, quit, and die.

So often when we are asked how things are going, we reply with answers like, "Man, I don't know if I'm going to make it through this season. I'm not sure I'm going to survive this semester. I don't know if I'm going to get through this time."

Have you ever heard yourself saying something like that? Where did you get that kind of thinking? Where did you hear those words of gloom and doubt? Not from your Good Shepherd. You likely heard them from the Enemy at your table.

See, your God has just told you that even though you walk through the valley of the shadow of death, you don't need to fear any evil. Did you catch the operative word in this sentence: *through*? Your Shepherd didn't just say you're going *to* the valley. He said you are going *through* the valley. In other words—you are going to make it.

That's "even though / I will" faith being developed in you. Even though times are tough, God's rod and staff are with you.

Even though times are hard, you are not alone. God knows you're going through a hard time. He knows the way is dark. He hasn't promised to deliver you from the trouble. He's promised to see you through the trouble. There's a big difference.

You will not find the Good Shepherd telling you that you're not going to make it. You will never find the Good Shepherd telling you that life is hopeless, there's no way out. Why not chuck it all, quit, and die? That is not the voice of the Good Shepherd. The Good Shepherd says, *We're going through this valley, and I'm going to be with you all the way through. And guess what—we're going to have a story to tell on the other side.*

This is how God delivered His people from bondage in Egypt. He didn't build a bridge over the Red Sea; He parted the sea so they could walk through it. Oftentimes God's plan is not to build a bridge over troubled waters. Instead, His miracle plan is to give you the grace and the power to miraculously go *through* the troubled waters. "Your road led through the sea, your pathway through the mighty waters—a pathway no one knew was there!" (Psalm 77:19 NLT). You are going *through* whatever circumstance you're currently in. And your Shepherd is going through it with you.

It's so easy to want to rewrite Psalm 23 so it says we sit at the table in God's presence only, and not in the presence of our enemies too. Christians talk about how they love the presence of God and long for the presence of God, and they pray things like, *Lord, would You just be with us today?* But guess what? God has already answered that prayer with a yes. "Do you not realize about yourselves, that Jesus Christ is in you?" the apostle Paul asked in 2 Corinthians 13:5 (ESV). We have an incarnational theology, which means that Jesus lives in us. There are moments when we sense that God is around us in a special or supernatural way. But we don't need to bank on the cloud or the fire that God's people saw manifested in days of old.

Interestingly, there isn't one verse in the New Testament that encourages us to seek or to celebrate the "presence" of God. Why? Because God is now made visible (and for the thirty-three years God was in human skin, tangible) in and through the person of Jesus, who now lives in us through the Spirit. I no longer seek the presence of Jesus. I seek the person of Jesus. I'm not after the presence of the Holy Spirit. I want the person of the Holy Spirit and His power. I'm not calling on the presence of God. I have God (Father, Son, and Spirit) living in me.

And God promises He is with us in the presence of our enemies. Jesus is at the table with us in the fire, in the hardship, in the feelings of hopelessness, in the broken world. God doesn't eliminate all of our difficulties. He allows us to walk through hardships, and He walks through those hardships with us.

Have you ever believed the lie that you're hopeless? You are not hopeless. Jesus lives in you! Don't give the Enemy a seat at your table.

THE LIE OF WORTHLESSNESS

Third, if you're hearing, *I'm not good enough*, the Enemy is at your table. Now, we've got to be really careful about this lie, because Scripture calls us to be humble. But as it's been well said: humility is not thinking less of yourself; humility is thinking of yourself less. We easily get these confused by thinking it honors God for us to think less of ourselves. But nothing could be further from the truth. You are made in the very image of God. That staggering reality doesn't cause us to strut around and grow an "it's all about me" persona. But it doesn't leave us wallowing in the misery of "I don't measure up to anything" either. These two outcomes are where the Devil wants to lead you. Either to an overinflated ego or to an underappreciated sense of just how significant and valuable you are.

In this instance, I'd love to encourage you if you tend to gravitate toward the latter camp—you just don't feel like you're enough. No matter what you've accomplished, or how much truth from God's Word you've heard over the years, you just don't believe you're enough.

Maybe someone told you you'd never amount to anything. Or maybe a spouse walked away. A parent bailed. Or the right man or woman you've longed for never walked through the door. Maybe you've always wished you looked like someone else. Or had the gifts that a friend has. Or maybe a dump truck of guilt backed into your story at some point and unloaded a pile of shame on you. No matter how hard you try, no matter what you do, in your mind it's never enough. And if you feel that way, certainly everyone else heartily agrees. Oh, sure, they're nice to your face. But you know how they really feel.

Here's the thing: you need to know the "not enough" anthem was composed in the pit of hell. It's crippling. Debilitating. Paralyzing. Suffocating. It didn't come from the Good Shepherd. If you're hearing it and repeating it, there must be an Enemy at your table.

This lie isn't a reflection of true humility. It's a club that beats you over the head. This lie whispers to you that you're useless. You will never have what it takes. Have you been called to lead a small group at your church? This lie insists it can't be done. Have you been called to lead your family with integrity and compassion and kindness and strength as a wife and mother who follows God? This lie tells you that you're not good enough; you're never going to amount to anything, so don't even bother trying. Do you believe that God loves you because He created you and calls you His beloved child? This lie tries to convince you that you're a spiritual reject. You're a worthless sinner who'll always be a worthless sinner. You're not God's child. He hates you.

Instead, look across the table. Lock eyes for a moment with the One who's sitting across from you. Do you see scorn and feel shame, or do you notice the scars on the hands that hold

THE HOLY ONE
INVITED YOU
HERE. BOOKED
THE TABLE.
PREPARED
THE MEAL. SAT
DOWN TO JOIN
YOU. AND THIS
RESERVATION
COST HIM
EVERYTHING.

———————————————

your water glass and the pitcher that's being lifted to fill it with a refreshing drink? Sure, Jesus is holiness personified, but the Holy One invited you here. Booked the table. Prepared the meal. Sat down to join you. And this reservation cost Him everything.

In the beautiful comparative picture we have of the Good Shepherd in John 10, Scripture tells us Jesus "lays down his life for the sheep" (v. 11). Jesus has put it all on the line to be sitting at the table with you! Don't give the Enemy a seat at your table.

THE LIE OF ME AGAINST THE WORLD

I was talking to a guy not long ago who told me he had just quit his job. I asked why. He said everybody hated him at the place he worked. He mentioned the company, and I'd thought he worked at a different company, so I named it. "No," he said. "I worked for the other company a few years back. I quit working there too. Everybody there was against me."

Sometime later I found out that he had left his wife. I asked him what happened, and he summed up their situation by saying, "Her parents never liked me from the start, and everyone in her family hated me."

Really? I thought.

When you believe the lie that everybody is against you, you are convinced everybody hates you. Everybody at your job hates you.

Everybody in your family hates you. Everybody in your church. Your pastors. Your professors. Your parents. Your children. Your friends. Your colleagues. Your neighbors. Even the waiter spit in your soup.

If you're hearing a voice that tells you, *Everybody is against you*, the Enemy is sitting at your table. It's the voice of fear-based illogic, of paranoia, a voice that encourages you to mistrust everybody in your life.

Certainly there are subtler forms of this lie. The Enemy is great at sowing seeds of doubt, at working to undermine your confidence about what God says is true about you. You might not exactly hear the word *hate*, but maybe you are hearing yourself say words like this: *Well, that person didn't even look up when I walked into the office—I bet she doesn't like me. See those people talking over there—I guarantee you they're talking about me. They are out to get me. Look at that friend—I bet she never wants to talk to me ever again. I don't have any friends. All my friends do things without me. No one ever invites me anywhere. Nobody likes me.*

What's the truth? Well, it's possible that somebody hates you. Sure. But it's not likely that *everybody*'s against you. What's more likely if you're hearing that lie is that you've got your fist clenched and you're ready to strike. Somewhere in the past you developed a defensive posture, an untrusting nature, and now it has become your default. Your walls are up. Tall and thick. Some might even call those walls impenetrable. People have hurt you in the past, so you're not going to let them ever get close to you again. You've taken a vow—whether spoken or unspoken—that you're going to punch people before they punch you. You're going to leave them before they ever leave you. You're going to slight them before they slight you. That's usually what's behind that lie.

The truth is that you need to let the Good Shepherd lead you by still waters. You need to let Him cause you to lie down in green pastures. You need to ask God to refresh your soul and guide you along righteous paths of healing and restoration for His name's sake. You may be surrounded by pressures and troubles and uncertainties and misunderstandings, but God has set a table for you in the middle of all this. God's got your back. Jesus is not some noodle-armed weakling. He's the Lord of all creation. All strength and power and authority belong to Him. He's King of the universe. When God is walking you through the valley, you can stop worrying about managing all the outcomes. You can stop looking over your shoulder. You can take the boxing gloves off.

Back in the season when I first received the *Don't give the Enemy a seat* text, I was speaking at a conference overseas. Some of the conference leaders and team circled up for prayer in a backstage room. They brought me and others leading in the next session to the center of the room. People circled us and laid their hands on us as a way of conferring Christ's power and provision on us.

After the prayer time ended, a woman I'd never met before walked up to me and began to quietly share something she sensed stirring in her spirit while we prayed. "Someone is trying to trip you up," she said. "But don't worry. God has your back." I got chills, given I was thousands of miles away from home and not a soul there knew about the struggle I was going through in our season of church planting. I've never forgotten that moment, and I repeat that phrase when I feel like the tide is turning against me. *Louie, don't worry. God has your back.*

Have you ever told yourself that truth, particularly in a tense time? When you and I remind ourselves of that truth, we're more prone to lay aside any fears, turn the attention off ourselves, and open our hands and hearts toward helping others.

The truth that God is for you and not against you matters greatly. If you don't believe this, you're constantly watching over your shoulder. This action of looking over your shoulder begins to create a false narrative, the image of a world in which you constantly play the victim card. You miss the freedom and encouragement of accepting the fact that people do love you. To be loved requires that you eventually agree with God and come to love yourself. It's a little scary at first if all you've ever known is a "me against the world" approach. But you weren't made to hate yourself. You were made to know that you're loved.

Sorry, but you can't reflect the bounty of all that's on your table if you're walking around with your fists clenched. Psalm 23 goes on to say in verse 5, "You anoint my head with oil; my cup runs over" (NKJV). The oily head part doesn't make much sense if you don't know much about sheep. The biggest nemesis for a sheep wasn't the big, bad wolf (although wolves were a threat, for sure) but tiny parasites and flies. The flies, little harbingers of aggravation, would attempt to lay their eggs in the soft tissue of the sheep's nose. Yuck. Can you imagine trying to breathe with a breeding factory for flies in your nostrils? The parasites would lodge themselves in the wool around the sheep's eyes and face, causing skin disease and irritation. So the shepherd would cover the sheep's head in oil. The oil provided a protective shield that prevented these irritants from finding safe harbor in the wool around the sheep's face and nose. God, through His Word, wants to protect you from aggravation, lies, and deceit.

But there's something else. Jesus wants your life to reflect the bounty of your table. He wants your life to overflow. Generosity is the calling card of everyone who dines regularly with the King. You don't hoard God's blessings. You pass out steak dinners to everyone around you. Even your enemies! Why? Because you can. You have more than enough on your table. You can lavishly share with everybody—even with those who might hate you. Generosity is impossible with closed fists. You can only give when you have open palms.

The table allows you to change the narrative from *Everybody hates me, everybody is against me* to *God is for me, God's got my back*. The bounty of the table changes you into an agent of love to those around you. You may be rejected by some. But you'll be surprised how many people around you are also waiting for someone to look up and reach out in love.

The Lord Almighty is for you. So everyone is not against you. Don't give the Enemy a seat at your table.

THE LIE THAT THERE'S NO WAY OUT

If you feel like you're surrounded and there's no way out, you know the Enemy is at your table.

This is a classic lie of the Enemy. It's that ultimate lie that combines several of the lies we've already addressed in this chapter. The Enemy convinces you there's nowhere to turn. Nowhere to run. No way forward. No chance you're ever going to live free again.

The consequences of your bad decisions are closing in from one side, the betrayal of a friend from another. Your reputation is toast. You're gonna lose your job. You can't go back to your community. You can't trust anyone. You've played your last card. The pressure is too great. Give up. Cash out. Get out of town, or worse, get out of this life.

I've been through enough storms to know the harsh reality of those feelings, so I'm not going to pretend following the advice

I'm giving you is a cakewalk. If you feel like you're surrounded and there's no way out, I've got game-changing news for you—you *are* surrounded! But it's better than you think.

Elijah, revered as one of the most powerful prophets in all Israel, was an anointed miracle worker who had called down fire on the prophets of false gods on Mount Carmel. At God's instruction Elijah passed on the anointing to young Elisha, a prophet and mighty man of faith, and he, too, walked in the power of God.

In a season of conflict and war, the king of Aram was bearing down on Israel, trying to take whatever shots he could to wreak destruction on the cities and the people of God. But God would tip Elisha off to the enemy king's plans. "Time and again Elisha warned the king [of Israel], so that he was on his guard in such places" (2 Kings 6:10). The king of Aram was ticked, and he wanted Elisha dead at all costs.

Elisha and his servant had traveled to a town called Dothan. When the king of Aram discovered that Elisha was the one feeding his battle plans to the king of Israel, he sent a massive force of men with chariots and horses to finish Elisha off. They arrived under the cover of darkness and surrounded the city while Elisha was sleeping.

The servant didn't sleep too well that night. Tossing and turning, every sound outside the camp unsettled him. Was someone there? Was danger lurking? Was Elisha safe? When morning broke the servant was already awake. He went out to survey the scene and couldn't believe what he saw. The town was completely surrounded. The Arameans had found Elisha's location and positioned themselves in a choking ring of assault during the night. There was no way out.

The servant rushed in to awaken Elisha. "Oh no, my lord! What shall we do?" (v. 15).

Elisha had a choice. Freak out. Fold. Or look up. Elisha chose to look up and lean into an "even though / I will" faith. He declared, "Those who are with us are more than those who are with them" (v. 16). And then he prayed. Not for himself. Not for deliverance from the pursuing army. Elisha prayed for his servant. Weird, no? Why would he do that?

Elisha prayed, "Open his eyes, LORD, so that he may see" (v. 17).

You might say the servant could see just fine. He could see well enough to recognize horse-drawn fighting chariots from a hundred yards away without corrective lenses. He could size up the hundreds of men and surmise that there was only himself and Elisha to stand against them. He could see well enough to know that they were boxed in, cornered.

What did he *not see* that prompted Elisha to pray this prayer?

He did not see that the army surrounding the city was itself surrounded by the angel army of the living God!

"The LORD opened the servant's eyes, and he looked and saw the hills full of horses and chariots of fire all around Elisha"

(v. 17). They were surrounded, all right. Surrounded by God-forces blazing with His glory and might.

The same is true for you and me. It may be true that circumstances are closing in. Enemies have taken up their positions in the night. Your whole world is surrounded by threats, accusations, missiles, and hate. But here's the thing: that's only half the story. The half you're getting from the adversary sitting at your table. He wants you to believe you are doomed. That there is no way out.

But the Spirit of God is interceding for you: *Lord, open her spiritual eyes; Father, let him see with the eyes of faith.*

God has everyone and everything that's surrounding you *surrounded.* Don't give the Enemy a seat at your table.

WHERE YOU WANT TO BE

When I had finally made the decision to ask Shelley to marry me, I was living in Fort Worth but headed home to Atlanta for Christmas break. Shelley was flying to Atlanta from Houston to spend a few days with my family, and I needed a ring.

Being in grad school and coming from a working middle-class family, I had to scrape and claw to get a suitable diamond. I got a break when a friend hooked me up with a dealer in the wholesale diamond mart in Dallas. I spent close to every penny I had on a beautiful stone. But it was a loose diamond, and I didn't have time to get it set in a ring before I headed home.

When you buy a diamond ring from a jewelry store, it comes in a velvet, flip-top box. But if you buy just a loose stone from an importer, you walk away with a precious gem wrapped in a small, folded piece of wax-type paper!

A few days later when I knelt down with the now set diamond and extended it toward Shelley, asking her to spend the rest of her life with me, I was holding the most valuable earthly possession I owned. Why? Shelley was worth it to me.

That's the beauty of the table God prepares for you. That's the wonder of the One who's waiting for you there right now. Jesus didn't send a message or a messenger to tell you how valuable you are. He came Himself. He paid the price. He is the prize. He's waited an eternity (literally) for you to join Him. And He's sitting across from you telling you that He thinks you are worth it.

When the Enemy tells you you're not smart enough, you're not strong enough, you don't have the right background, you're not pretty enough, you don't matter enough . . . look up and lock eyes with the King. Hear Him say, *Daughter—Son—there's nowhere I'd rather be than at this table with you*. His words are the words of life (John 6:68). His voice thunders from heaven (Psalm 68:33). His voice drowns out every Enemy lie. By His grace, you can start taking authority over the voices at your table and kick the Devil out of your dinner party. He has to flee in Jesus' name.

FIVE

SPIRAL OF SIN

Adjustments are needed.

For much of the last decade I had the privilege of serving in ministry alongside my friend Chette Williams, the chaplain of the Auburn University football team, a team I have loved since I was a kid. Being up close to the team, watching the way Chette served and encouraged the players, coaches, and staff, was a dream come true. Walking beside these young men in good days and hard ones was an honor.

My role was to be a friend to the team. A support. Yet, as a student of the game, I particularly loved to be with the players and coaches in the locker room at halftime. As a fan in the stands, you don't get the true inside view of what's happening with the team. At halftime, you might be happy that your favorite player rushed for a bunch of yards. Or you might feel confident about a win knowing your team is up by three touchdowns. But in the locker room, you see a powerful recalibration happening among the team.

The coaches have a multidimensional view of the game. They have eyes on the defense and offense of their own team, and they know their own team's playbook inside and out. But they've also studied the opposing team by watching countless hours of film from their previous games. They know the opponent's tendencies in every situation. The coaches understand the big picture.

So it's halftime, and the players jog into the locker room. They grab some water and down some quick energy snacks. The real work begins. The offense and defense huddle on opposite sides of the locker room. Coaches project slides on the wall or draw on a whiteboard, and one of the coaches says, "Okay, whenever we are doing XYZ play, they are running ABC defense against us. They're putting these two guys over here, and that guy over there, and they look like they're going to run this direction, but they're really running that direction. That's what's stopping us. Here's what we're going to do. When they do ABC, we're going to do 123. We might have played one way in the first half, but here's how we're going to play in the second half."

Great coaching (and most often, victory) is about making the right adjustments.

Consider this moment right now. You were created in the

image of God. You were called to greatness. You are God's workmanship, a child of the King, and God wants to set you free from anything that's holding you back. God wants you to live in the fullest potential that He has for your life. It's time you got serious about victory now that God has given you the opportunity to ask, *How is the opposition coming against me? What is the Enemy doing to me? What adjustments can be made?* You can win the battle for your mind.

UNCHECKED THOUGHTS

It's adjustment time. Soberly and honestly examine if you've given the Devil a seat at your table. Consider what Psalm 23 has promised you, as we've discussed: Jesus has prepared a table for you in the presence of your enemies. The pressure of life is all around you, yet your Almighty God has invited you to sit and dine. Whenever you allow the Devil to sit, he worms his way into a dinner party that belongs to you and God alone. The Enemy begins to devour the abundant life meant for you. He's eating your lunch, so to speak. You start heading down the pathway toward sin and death.

Death, in this sense, is spiritual death—not eternal condemnation for believers, but the destruction of the close relationship you are meant to fully and deeply enjoy with God. Scripture is clear that nothing separates you from God's love (Romans 8:38–39), yet followers of Christ can still grow distant from God if they so choose. If the Devil sits at your table, sin can fill your mind and sour your conscience and ruin the intimate harmony you enjoy with the Lord. With sin in your life, you lose your peace, effectiveness, confidence, and cheerfulness. Relationships are strained. You don't live to your fullest God-given potential.

Complicating matters, your own thoughts and feelings can combine with sin and temptation in a spiral that goes around and around. Maybe you've noticed a tendency for people to repeat the same sins. Maybe you've noticed that in your own life. Sometimes the spiral is generational, where the harmful patterns of your grandparents' behavior and attitudes were passed along to your parents, and now you see them showing up in your own life and in the lives of your kids. Other times, the spiral is personal. When life gets tough, we return to our familiar sins, even though we know they're harmful. Either way, the spiral needs to be broken. That's why it's helpful for us to be aware of how this spiral works so we can combat the Enemy's schemes (2 Corinthians 2:11).

The spiral begins this way: a temptation or thought that's not from God comes into your mind. Stop right there. Identify that reality. If a harmful thought enters your mind, it's not from God. We must be awakened to this. Those thoughts are from the Enemy, who often uses our own desires against us. How? James 1:13–15 describes the start of the spiral this way: "Let no one say when he is tempted, 'I am being tempted by God,' for God cannot be tempted with evil, and he himself tempts no one. But each person is tempted when he is lured and enticed by his own desire. Then desire when it has conceived gives birth to sin, and sin when it is fully grown brings forth death" (ESV).

We are "lured" and "enticed" by our own desires. That means the Enemy has a plan for your life and mine, and his plan is to bury us. You and I aren't living in a vacuum, making neutral choices. We live on a battlefield. We're stamped with the image of God and targeted by the Enemy who uses our own desires against us, as James says. Our Enemy hates God and wants to destroy everything he can that bears God's image. Be aware of this! The Enemy wants to kill your dreams. He wants to bury the purpose God has placed inside of you. He wants to steal your sense of self-worth and confidence and hope. He wants to destroy your marriage and erode your relationship with your kids. He wants to ruin your good reputation and slander the name of Christ in the process. He's got all kinds of time and no mercy. The way he's going to start you down this road of destruction is by putting a thought into your mind that's contrary to God's best for your life and letting it entice you and fester.

Despite the Enemy's malicious intent, I don't want you to be fearful or paranoid. First John 4:4 says, "Greater is He who is in you than he who is in the world" (NASB). That's a verse you need to remember. I also don't want you to become overly obsessed with the Devil, thinking every bad thing that happens in your life is coming directly from him. If you're trying to get to work in the morning and your car won't start, you're most likely not going to get to work sooner by casting Satan out of your car engine. What you need are some jumper cables. It's just a dead battery.

Yet you also can't go through life with blinders on, thinking the world is a neutral place. You have a real Enemy, and he's putting harmful thoughts into your head all the time, with the ultimate goal of wiping you out. One of the biggest ways he works at doing that is with unchecked thoughts. That's what needs to be stopped. That's why we need this halftime adjustment.

FISHING LESSONS

Sin can look so good at first. Helpful even. We're apt to believe that the tempting thoughts in our minds are a solution to the pressures we face. But watch out.

We know from Ezekiel 28:12–17 that Satan was originally a high-ranking angel who rebelled against God and was cast out from heaven. Isaiah 14:12 describes how Satan was cast out of heaven like a star falling to the ground. Your foe is somebody to take seriously—and his nature is deceptive and misleading. Genesis 3:1 describes the evil one as "more crafty" than any other created thing. That means he's cunning, deceitful, fraudulent. He runs the spiritual equivalent of a shell game—showing you where the little ball is hidden at first, then slip-sliding the cups around so you always come up losing.

The Devil never rolls through the front door of your life announcing he's going to destroy you. He doesn't show you a picture of yourself eighteen months from now living alone in a rented room because you've lost your most trusted relationships. He doesn't direct your attention to a PowerPoint presentation of clear, step-by-step plans of how he's going to bring you to your destruction. Instead, he slips through the side door. He lures and entices you. It's like fishing.

You'd never hop into your boat, row out to the middle of the lake, and whip out a bullhorn: "Attention! Hey there, fish! Listen up. I'm going to throw a razor-sharp hook overboard. You need to bite it. I'm going to jerk the line really hard, reel you in, and yank out the hook with pliers. The hook has a barb on its end, and your mouth is going to be a mess. I'm going to throw you in a cooler. I'll take you back to shore where I'll scrape your scales off, cut out your insides, and fry you over the fire in a buttered pan. Any questions? Let's go!"

Nope. When you go fishing you get crafty. You check the temperature and wind speed and the lay of shadow on the water. You consult other fishermen and pull out your tackle box and select the perfect lure for the lake and type of fish. The hook is never obvious. Never scary. Lures are shiny. Brightly colored.

They spin. They announce, "Free lunch!" and "Really cool thing over here!" A fisherman wants to mesmerize a fish. He wants to tantalize it. He needs the fish to pursue the dazzling lure, eyes and mouth wide open. The fisherman never advertises the hook. He advertises the reward. His big goal is to get Mr. Largemouth Bass to bite.

The Devil holds the fishing pole. We have to constantly watch out for the Devil's lures. When that temptation or harmful thought comes our way, it's probably not going to look bad—not at first. Initially it promises something good. Sin offers a solution. Sin guarantees relief. If you're down, sin brings you up. If you're stuck, sin shows the way out. If you're miserable, sin promises comfort. If you're outraged, sin offers the perfect justice. If you're lonely, sin becomes your best friend.

All lies.

All that feigned goodness, all those false solutions, all the relief, all the comfort, all the justice, all the camaraderie. All those promises are meaningless. Sin is not your pal, and sin is not your buddy. Sin is not on your side. Sin doesn't have your back. Sin is never the magic elixir it claims to be. Sin is a mirage, always overpromising and underdelivering.

The Enemy works in your life by luring and lying. He promises things he can't fulfill. He challenges God's truth. He attacks God's character and intentions. The Enemy says things such as, *Surely God's holding out on you—you can't trust Him.* He essentially told

Eve, *If you eat from this fruit, your eyes are going to be opened; you're going to be like God.* The Enemy appeals to your basic human needs. We all have the need for acceptance, worth, satisfaction, fulfillment, and happiness. The Enemy constantly holds out a lure and offers a lie: *Hey, this will satisfy your needs. Take a bite. You deserve to be happy.*

Mixed with this, the Enemy often uses other people to encourage our hasty choices. Sometimes we need to change our circle of friends because they're in the habit of rolling out the red carpet for us when it comes to doing dumb things. Maybe you're in the elevator with the wrong people. Instead of taking you up to God things, they take you down to the basement of defeat because that's where they're living. Misery loves company. And miserable people have a way of wanting those around them to fail, not succeed.

Don't fall for the lies. Don't chase the lure. Don't give the Enemy a seat at your table.

HAND-TO-HAND COMBAT

I need to clarify that when a harmful thought or temptation first enters your mind, that is not sin—not in and of itself. Jesus was tempted. The Enemy sent harmful thoughts His way. The Devil actually spoke to Jesus in the wilderness (Matthew 4:1–11), and Jesus heard the Devil's words, yet Jesus never chose to entertain the Devil's voice. See, when a harmful thought or temptation comes into our minds, we have a choice. We can either discard that thought or entertain it. If we discard it, good. But if we entertain it, that's when the Devil sits at our table. The sin happens when we keep hold of that harmful thought and let it take root in our minds.

Jesus taught this in the Sermon on the Mount. All sorts of folks were entertaining unhealthy thoughts, although they weren't acting on those thoughts. They figured all was well. But in Matthew 5:21–22 and 27–28, Jesus came along and blew this up. *Hey*, He told them, *you think you're doing fine because you're not actually murdering people. Well, guess what? If you simply hate somebody enough to want them dead . . . that's as bad as murder. You might think you're fine because you're not actually in bed with someone you're not married to, but guess what? If you're merely imagining yourself in an illicit relationship with someone, that's also wrong. You're committing sin with that person in your heart.*

Entertaining a harmful thought is as bad as doing a harmful deed. That's key because it's far too easy to think we're not sinning merely because we're not acting on a sinful thought. Here's the fact: the thought itself falls short of the glory of God. When we entertain it, the thought muddies our relationship with the Lord. The thought itself occupies our mind and has the power to knock us off course. Romans 12:2 gives this stiff warning: "Don't copy the behavior and customs of this world, but let God transform you into a new person by *changing the way you think.* Then you will learn to know God's will for you, which is good and pleasing and perfect" (NLT, italics added).

The frightening reality is this: once we let a harmful thought pitch a tent in our mind, eventually that temptation is acted on.

Period.

Sometimes people insist that harmful thoughts don't always lead to harmful actions, but I disagree. Harmful actions always begin with harmful thoughts, and harmful thoughts, harbored over time, always lead to harmful actions. Those thoughts must be stopped. If those thoughts are entertained long enough, they will win the battle for your mind.

Sometimes we will actually do the harmful thing that we're thinking about, while at other times the shift is simply that our attitude toward the sinful choice changes. We slowly warm up to sin. Either way, the harmful thoughts have led us to being negatively influenced. If you're thinking about committing adultery, maybe you will actually commit adultery. Or perhaps, after repeatedly imagining yourself committing adultery, you're more willing to conclude that adultery isn't that bad. Adultery is beneficial. Adultery opens doors for you. Adultery is the solution to your marital problems. All lies.

Because this is truth, too, and this is why the Enemy's lures are so dangerous: sin usually feels good. Just for a moment. We often skip over this part of the story in church, but it needs to be told if we're to be aware of the Enemy's schemes. Sin can be fun—at least for a little while. Proverbs 14:12–13 lays this out plainly. "There's a way of life that looks harmless enough; look again—it leads straight to hell. Sure, those people appear to be having a good time, but all that laughter will end in heartbreak" (THE MESSAGE). Can I get an amen? That description in Proverbs sounds like many people's weekends. *Man, we were laughing so hard. We were having such an amazing time. But whoa, the next morning I was so miserable.*

Moses grew up as the son of Pharaoh's daughter. He had all the opportunity to enjoy the privileges of life in the Egyptian palace. Yet Hebrews 11:25 says that Moses chose not "to enjoy the fleeting pleasures of sin." He went the other direction. The pleasures of sin are enjoyable, but they are not *lasting* pleasures, and they are certainly not pleasures that honor God. Sinful pleasures don't provide peace or fulfillment. They lead to harm, separation, disappointment, and shame.

That's how it works. The Devil shows you a lure. You bite the lure, but it doesn't deliver what was promised. Instead, you end up in a downward sin spiral into shame, separation, and destruction.

SIN IS NEVER THE SOLUTION

Sometimes people say they hate going to church because church makes them feel guilty. But people don't feel bad because a preacher tells them to. They feel bad on their own. God has created us to be like Him, and when we miss the mark, a negative effect happens in our souls. When we sin, we feel frustrated. Guilty. Ashamed. It's because we are falling short of what God intended us to be. The frustration often lies within ourselves. We grit our teeth and mutter, "Man, I can't believe I did that again. I can't believe I went there again."

It's that crazy spiral at work. We started out by feeling some sort of loss or experiencing some kind of trouble. We didn't feel great. We sought relief. The Enemy was nearby, moving quickly. We spotted the forbidden fruit he offered us. The fruit didn't look bad. We mulled over the idea for a while, and maybe we wondered why God withheld that fruit from us in the first place. Maybe God didn't love us after all. So we acted on our thoughts and bit into the fruit. The fruit tasted good for one brief moment. The chunk slid down our gullet, and then we realized we were naked. We were ashamed of what we'd done.

So we're right back where we started. Feeling some sort of loss. Experiencing some kind of trouble. Not feeling great. Only now, that misery is compounded by shame. We feel worse than we did before.

Let me lay this pattern out plainly. If you're feeling lousy and you sin in an attempt to feel better, whatever pain you're feeling right now will still be there tomorrow morning, only worse. If you get a poor review from your supervisor, that hurts. But if you think the solution is to get drunk, guess what? The sting of your poor review will still be there tomorrow morning. You'll also be hungover with a killer headache.

In that moment of misery, one more turn of the spiral usually occurs. After sin happens, and when we're feeling miserable and ashamed, the Enemy shifts tactics. All the way up until now, he's been whispering to you, *See the fruit? Take the fruit. The fruit looks good, doesn't it? God has been denying you this fruit. God never said you shouldn't have this fruit. I promise you, if you eat this fruit, this is going to solve your problem.* But as soon as you eat the fruit and hit guilt, shame, and frustration, the Enemy changes roles. He shifts from being the enticer and promiser to becoming the accuser and the condemner.

Now he's all over your case. He's telling you that you're the dumbest person he's ever seen. He insists you're the poorest example of a Christian there's ever been. *If there's ever a Christian who didn't get it, that's you. You're hopeless. A complete failure. Man, you really messed up this time. God hates you. He's angry with you. You idiot. You're so far gone, you'll never get back. Let's watch a replay of what you just did, okay? It's hilarious because you're so pathetic.*

Far too often we let him accuse us. We know we've done wrong, so we just mumble our agreement right along with the Enemy. The same Enemy who once enticed us with a promise is now crushing us with an accusation—and we agree with him. *That's right. I messed up again, and I know it. I know I'm pathetic.*

Instead, we should be screaming, "Shut up! You are the one

who tried to convince me this was a great idea. I'm done with you. I am a child of God, a new creation, and even when I sin those facts don't change." See, if the Enemy can accuse you of sin, he can condemn you, and this is the ultimate blow. When he reaches the point of condemnation, the Enemy has just pronounced a judgment on you. *You're unworthy. You're finished. You're a complete failure. You have no more value. You have no more worth. You have no more future.* Have you ever noticed how government officials condemn buildings before they smash them to the ground?

That's what the Enemy wants to do to you. He wants to flatten you to rubble. If he can accuse you, he can condemn you. And if he can condemn you, he can destroy you. *The little feeble Christian just sinned again*, he whispers, rubbing his hands in glee. *Bring on the wrecking ball.*

Here's good news: one huge difference between God and Satan is that the Enemy will condemn you, but God will convict you. There's a world of difference between the two actions. Condemnation is done from a posture of hate. Conviction is done from a posture of love.

THIS TIME IT'S GOING TO BE DIFFERENT

When we struggle in sin, God does not take our sin neutrally. He convicts us of our shortcomings, but He only does so because

He cares about us. He loves us so much He doesn't want us to continue down a harmful path. If you feel the need to pivot in your thought life, you're feeling the need for repentance, and that prompt is from God. God longs to restore you. But if you feel that you are worthless and may as well drop out and quit, that you're hopeless and a complete failure—that thinking came from the Enemy. You need to be careful to listen to the right voice. Here's what those two voices look like:

Condemnation comes from guilt.
Conviction is born out of grace.

Condemnation leads you to conceal your sin.
Conviction urges you to confess it.

Condemnation results in remorse (feeling bad about what you did).
Conviction calls you to repentance (turning to go the other way).

Condemnation prompts you to rededicate.
Conviction demands full surrender.

Condemnation is a path to future failure.
Conviction is a highway to real change.

I grew up in a spiritual culture where "rededications" were the norm. Maybe you did too. If you're not familiar with what I'm referring to, here's what was common at youth camp and church meetings. After the message, the music would play, the choir would sing, and the preacher would give an invitation for anybody to be saved. He'd wait a while, and if nobody came forward, then the music would keep playing and the choir would keep singing, and he'd give another invitation for anyone who wanted to rededicate their life to God to come forward. He'd usually get a couple of folks then. If it was the fourth night of youth camp, the altar would be flooded with people and tears.

The call for rededications was a well-meaning call. The preacher was acknowledging that people go astray and that God's grace provides second chances. If you've gone astray, there's always hope for you. You can come back to God. The people in the pews who came forward to rededicate their lives were acknowledging God's mercy. They were believers, but they'd sinned and fallen short of God's glory. Now they were seeking repentance and restoration. That was good.

But I'm not a fan of rededications. Why? Because I've walked forward more than once and promised God that this was going to be the last time, somehow thinking in the emotion of the moment I had the strength to change my story on my own. I've been to that church service. I've been to that youth group. I've

**CONDEMNATION
IS A PATH
TO FUTURE
FAILURE.
CONVICTION IS
A HIGHWAY TO
REAL CHANGE.**

---

been to that retreat. I've written my sins on a piece of paper and thrown them into the campfire or nailed them to a cross erected at the camp. I drew a line in the sand with the stick and snapped my stick like Christ snaps the yoke of sin.

Ever do something similar? Maybe it wasn't at a retreat or a conference. Maybe you just got down on your knees and said, "Dear Lord, I promise if You forgive me this time, I will never, ever, ever do that sin again." Then you got up and sighed with relief. Whew, you rededicated that one. Then the next week you got on your knees again and said, "Lord, I know that last time I said I'd never do that again. Well, I did. But things are different now. I promise. This time I really mean it. If You'll forgive me one more time, I swear to You that this is the last time."

I'm not ripping on the church culture that shaped my youth. But I am challenging us to take a long, hard look at rededication culture, because it's far too easy to fall into the pattern of rededicating the rededication. Sin happens, and you promise things are going to change. You grit your teeth and ask for God's forgiveness, and you promise things are going to be different next time. But then you fall again. So you get up and dust yourself off and confess your sin and rededicate your life again. *I promise. I swear. I vow. I pledge. You have my word, God. This is the last time. Honest!*

Rededications are so often packed with the impossible promise that we'll never sin again. The big problem with rededications is that they can reflect our efforts to clean up our own lives. We make the vow. We do the pledge. We promise to God what we will do to change. And, sorry, but our earnest promises aren't good enough to cause lasting change. Here's a big danger: we rededicate our rededications so often we reach the point of hopelessness. We conclude nothing's ever going to change. Something must be wrong with the gospel. Or something must be wrong with us.

Far too many Christians check out of church right there. *Faith didn't work, so I'm going to abandon my faith. God didn't change me, so forget God.* At the bottom of the spiral, we find ourselves vulnerable, weak, and isolated. We feel empty and desperate. So we hide. We hide from our friends. We hide from God. Our unarticulated goal (and it's nothing new) is the false hope that we will become invisible to God. He's walking in the cool of the evening in the garden of Eden, longing to talk with us like He's done in the past, but we're going to hide ourselves with fig leaves in a frail attempt to avoid Him. If God's walking one way, we're going the other direction.

Hiding is one of the worst things we can do. If you're hiding from God, you've fallen for another ploy of the Enemy. He's at your table, and he's eaten most of your meal by now. You're feeling all the symptoms of malnutrition and starvation in your emotions, your relationships, and your spirit. The unmet longing that got you into the mess in the first place is exposed again. You need love. You need peace. You need understanding. You need worth, significance, purpose, and fulfillment in your life. You're right back where you started. That's when the Enemy places his shiny fishing lure in front of you again and says, *Hey, you need some pleasure. Remember how good you felt—at least for a moment—the last time when we went down this road? Let's do it again.* Here comes the same harmful thought trying to pitch a tent in your mind. No, the solution is not another rededication.

The solution is surrender.

Surrender comes when we raise our hands and say, "God, obviously I can't do anything to change this situation. But Jesus, You can. I'm not going to hide from You anymore. I'm going to open my heart up to Your love and Your solutions and to the investigative and restorative work of the Holy Spirit. I'm going to follow You and Your leadership, Jesus. You have finished the work on the cross, and You have ultimately won this war. There might be battles left for me to fight, but You've established a beachhead of victory for me on the shore. Thanks to Your victory, I can go forward. I'm going to open myself up to the hard work of having You create the change in my life. I'm going to pray this in the power that God used to raise You from the dead. That's what I want, and I surrender my life—and this particular problem—to You."

This is resurrection power at work, and this is how God invites us to victory. It's fantastic news! Jesus makes it possible for us to reject the spiral of temptation and sin. God's promise to us is found in 1 Corinthians 10:12–13: "No temptation has overtaken you except what is common to mankind. And God is faithful; he will not let you be tempted beyond what you can bear. But when you are tempted, he will also provide a way out so that you can endure it."

Think about that for a moment.

God. Will. Provide. A. Way. Out.

That's bedrock truth. A promise to you from Almighty God. We don't need to allow the Enemy to pull up a seat at our table. We can live lives of victory. We can win the battle for our minds.

SIX

FREEDOM REVOLUTION

Imagine hiking in a swampy area. The going is tough, and you're all alone. You keep a watchful eye out for predators, but you don't notice that you've suddenly strayed into some sandy-looking terrain. The ground feels spongy for one step. Two. Suddenly it gives way.

You're up to your knees in quicksand.

It's wet. Shifting. You're stuck and very slowly going down. You shout for help, but no one's around. You fight to free yourself, but you can't reach any handholds to lift yourself up. You struggle. You flail against the wet sand, but you're soon up to your thighs and slowly continuing to sink. You're trapped. Definitely panicking now.

An hour goes by. Another hour. Still another. The sun is

scorching hot overhead. You vow not to give up, but you're growing exhausted. The harder you fight, the more the quicksand weighs you down. You've heard somewhere that struggling only makes you sink faster, so you try to be still, but it's against all your instincts. You flounder. Grasp for anything. The grit of the murky sand chafes against your skin. You're past your waist now, your body firmly wedged in the trap. Another hour goes by. Another. You're down past your chest. You barely have the energy to kick anymore. You can hardly move.

Here's a startling fact about quicksand: due to the physics of shifting sand and weight distribution, the grains of sand that trap you almost always jam up and bind together before you sink too far. It's a phenomenon called "force chain,"[1] and unlike what you see in the movies, you won't be suddenly sucked in over your head. In the real world, you can sink a long way down, particularly if you struggle, and you definitely can die in quicksand. Yet people seldom die from sinking and suffocating, as you might think. Instead, they die from exhaustion. From the effects of desperation and exposure.

They die because they wear themselves out trying to escape.

When it comes to fighting sin, the same can be true. Many of us are floundering in poor choices; for years we've battled against the spiral of sin and temptation as though it were quicksand, but it keeps sucking us down. We keep struggling, but we can't seem to climb onto solid ground. In desperation we panic or lapse into spiritual exhaustion. It seems no matter what we try, we can't free ourselves, and it feels like we've reached the point where we can't fight anymore. We're an inch from giving up. But guess what?

You do not need to be swallowed in the quicksand of sin.

SURROUNDED, CLOTHED, SECURE, NEW

You have victory in Christ. This is not mere preacher-talk or church rhetoric. Jesus has already won. He's seated in the place of victory at the right hand of God (Hebrews 12:2). When eternity unfolds, Jesus won't return to earth to fight sin again. He'll return as the ultimate victor. Because Jesus has already won the victory over sin, you have access to this victory too. You are freed from sin's quicksand by living in your new identity. Sin, temptation, and a poor thought life don't need to hold you down. The power to live freely comes from your close association with Christ and His victory.

To be clear, our battle isn't won because the pressure lifts from our lives or because our circumstances change. We've seen this all along in our study of Psalm 23:4–5. We will still walk through dark valleys throughout our entire lives. We will still sit at a table that's surrounded by enemies. The battle isn't won because the pressure lets up. No. The battle is won because of who walks with us through the dark valleys and who sits at the table with us when we're surrounded by troubles.

What does it mean to be associated with Christ and His victory? Let's unpack this concept. Second Corinthians 5:17 says we are "in Christ" and a "new creation," and Galatians 3:26–28 says we are "clothed" with Christ. It means that Jesus makes us brand new, and we're completely enfolded by the righteousness of Christ. Colossians 3:3 talks about how our lives are "hidden with Christ." Imagine a hidden room in a house, or a hidden pocket inside a coat. When something is hidden, it's both concealed and secure. Our brand-new righteousness isn't fleeting. It's protected and safe. Train your mind and heart to believe that you are a new creation. Your righteousness is safe because of Christ.

There's more. Ephesians 2:6 says, "God raised us up with Christ and seated us with him in the heavenly realms." That means we are united with Christ in victory. Since Christ was brought up from the grave, we are brought up together with Him also. We are *that* closely connected with Christ. Whatever Jesus has won, we have won also. God Almighty took on the form of a human who took the full weight of the world's sins on the cross. Jesus suffered and died and was raised to life again. That is what has won the battle. First Corinthians 15:57 says, "Thanks be to God! He gives us the victory through our Lord Jesus Christ." Train your mind and heart to see yourself as victorious in Christ.

When temptations threaten us, we first become free by changing our perspectives. Instead of floundering in the quicksand of sin and temptation for the rest of our lives, we change how we think. We take responsibility for what happens in our minds and say, "I am in Christ, and Christ is in me. I am a brand-new creation. Christ is the victor, and I can adopt a mindset that sees me walking in all the victory Jesus has won for me."

Your new mindset tells you that God is faithful. You remind yourself of this truth. You remind yourself and remind yourself again. That constant reminding begins to change the old patterns that led you to defeat. Sin is not the end of the story anymore. Your faithful God promised a way out of temptation. True to His promise, He provides the way out, so you can and will escape this temptation. You can walk through dark valleys, and you can sit in the presence of your enemies with a different way of thinking about what God has for you. First John 5:4 says, "Everyone born of God overcomes the world. This is the victory that has overcome the world."

How do you refuse the Enemy a seat at your table? You must start from this place of identity. You remind yourself that Jesus has already won your struggle. And because you are joined with Him, something powerful has already happened. Whatever He has won, you have won. You are in Christ, and Christ is in you. Since Christ has victory, you have access to that victory right now. You're not fighting the battle against sin on your own strength. You're tapping into the huge, all-powerful engine of God's resurrection power (Philippians 3:10). This is that engine for change we hinted at earlier.

Maybe that sounds like a lot of theological rhetoric to get your mind around, but it really isn't complicated. It boils down to God's faithfulness. Let's look again at 1 Corinthians 10:13: "No temptation has overtaken you except what is common to mankind. And God is faithful; he will not let you be tempted beyond what you can bear. But when you are tempted, *he will also provide a way out* so that you can endure it" (italics added).

It's that straightforward. Read the verse again.

God is faithful.

When you rely on Him, He will provide a way out.

SAINT (YOUR NAME GOES HERE)

Let's reinforce the application. Whenever you face temptation, it's like you're staring at a big closed door. The door is unlocked, and on the other side of the door is sin—some sort of harmful living. Many believers stare at that big door and don't think they have any power to keep the door shut. They believe they must open the door marked Temptation and walk through it. They don't feel like they have a choice. Part of the reason for this faulty thinking is because we have flawed identity theology present in today's church.

Here's the big revelation. We are *not* simply sinners saved by grace. We must change this distorted thinking. We are *not* simply beggars helping other beggars find bread. We have *not* simply come to the cross with nothing to offer. This may be the starting point, but this is not the whole story and is not our true identity if we are in Christ. We are *not* just a big bunch of sinners. Yet the problem is, too often, we hear this—and variations of it—over and over in today's churches.

Hi, welcome to church today. We're so glad you're here. Please sit down and enjoy today's sermon. Never forget you're a sinner—that's all you are. You came to Jesus with empty hands, and that's all you'll ever offer Him. You're just clutching filthy rags. You're a worm. A wretch. A mocker. A scoffer. Unclean. Unworthy. You're always in rebellion against God. You are utterly devoid of value. You're only a sinner saved by grace, and if you ever forget it, just remember how you sinned yesterday, you sinned today, and how you're going to sin tomorrow. You sinned this morning, and you sinned last night, and you sinned ten minutes ago. That's all you'll ever do. Thank you. Okay, let's stand and sing. See you again next Sunday.

It sounds pious and humble, but it's a load of rot. It's horrible identity theology. With teaching like that, it's hard to do anything else except nod and mumble, "Yeah, I guess that's true." Then when you walk up to the big door marked Temptation, you don't stand a chance. You open the door and walk through it since that's what you've been conditioned to do. You don't think you have any options except to wallow in the sin on the other side because you've been following a partial gospel.

When we walk up to the door marked Temptation—and I really want to drive this point home—we need to preach to ourselves equal parts Ephesians 2:8–9 and 2 Corinthians 5:17. That's the full gospel. We were sinners saved by grace at the start of our salvation experience, as Ephesians 2:8–9 points out. Yet that's not the end of the story. That's why you can't pitch a tent in the sinner campground anymore. Your new identity is a sinner saved by grace who is a brand-new creation, as 2 Corinthians 5:17 points out. The old has passed away. The new you has arrived. You were born again to a brand-new life, and in Jesus Christ you are not the same as who you were before you got saved.

Christians often point to Jeremiah 17:9 and say, "Well, look. It says right there that the heart is deceitful above all else and desperately wicked. So that's who I am. That's me. I've got a deceitful heart, and I'm desperately wicked."

What some may have missed is how the Bible uses that verse to describe an unregenerate heart, a heart that's still far from God. But Jesus has ushered in a new era. True, after we begin to follow Christ, our hearts are still capable of sinning, yet Jesus has made them brand new. In Ezekiel 36:26 God said, "I will give you a new heart and put a new spirit in you; I will remove from you your heart of stone and give you a heart of flesh." That means our hearts are not desperately wicked and prone to deceit anymore.

We get confused on this issue because even after we are new creations, we still have the capacity to sin. No one needs that sermon; we know it too well. Yet we must continually tell ourselves that "sinner" is no longer our identity. So when we stare at the door marked Temptation, we need to remind ourselves that we were crucified with Christ and don't need to live the way we used to.

The life you now live is by faith, and you live because Christ lives in you (Galatians 2:20). When you became a believer, you were baptized into Christ Jesus—which means you identified with His death, burial, and resurrection. Just as Christ was raised from the dead by the glory of the Father, you too "walk in newness of life" (Romans 6:4 ESV). That's who you are today! You don't need to go through the door marked Temptation.

In short, you remind yourself you're a saint. Does it surprise you that the Bible calls you a saint?[2] Maybe you hear that word and think, *Nah, my grandma is a saint. Me on the other hand? That's a little dicey.* But it's true. This is how you are referred to in Scripture. The word *saint* simply means that you are a "holy one." There are more than forty verses in the New Testament that call us saints. In Christ, you're forgiven of all sin—past, present, and future. You have a righteous standing before God. You are clothed by the righteousness of Jesus Christ. Don't walk through the door marked Temptation. You're a saint.

ALWAYS A WAY OUT

I can hear questions already. You're saying, *Yeah, but Louie, what about Paul? In 1 Timothy 1:15, he said, "Here is a trustworthy saying that deserves full acceptance: Christ Jesus came into the world to save sinners—of whom I am the worst." Even the great apostle Paul called himself the chief of sinners. If that was Paul's identity, what hope do I have?*

We have to understand the broader context. That was not Paul's identity. Paul was saying, *If you line up all the folks who couldn't make it without the grace of God, then I need to be put at the top of that list. If you're trying to find people who need God's grace to cover sin, then I'm in the number one spot.*

Paul's more complete declaration is found in Romans 6:1–2. He asked, "What shall we say, then? Shall we go on sinning so that grace may increase? By no means! We are those who have died to sin; how can we live in it any longer?"

The statement is emphatic. By no means! Paul was tough on this practical issue. *Should we just keep going through the door marked Temptation,* Paul asked, *around and around in a circle, so we can experience the wonderful grace of God? Is that the way we should live? More sin, more grace, more sin, more grace? No way!* he shouted, to answer his own question. "By no means!" He went on to explain how "just as Christ was raised from the dead through the glory of the Father, we too may live a new life"

(Romans 6:4). This is where the victory starts: by immersing yourself in the truth that you are a new creation. You are no longer a slave to sin. God will provide a way out. You have the victory in Christ. You do not have to give the Enemy a seat at your table.

If you've been to London, maybe you've taken a ride on the London Underground, the city's subway system. It's often referred to by its nickname, "the Tube." What's amazing is that different lines run at different depths under the surface of the ground. Maybe you start on the Jubilee line, then transfer to the Piccadilly line, then go to the Central line, then travel for a while on the Bakerloo line. If it's not your everyday commute, you can get disoriented, especially given that all these different train lines operate at differing levels below ground. The deepest levels are the two platforms of the Jubilee line at London Bridge, which run 23.2 meters below sea level, or 76.11 feet.[3] You're almost eight stories underground. When you're down there, other trains are whizzing overhead. This can all be quite confusing.

But here's the good news for a guy from Atlanta: everywhere you go in the Underground, you see signs that say Way Out. The signs themselves don't look the same, but they all say the same thing. I took pictures of a bunch of different signs last time we were there. One sign was round with a red circle around it. Another sign was long, thin, rectangular, and blue. Another sign was scripted inside the shape of a stained-glass window. Another was pure business. No matter the shape or color of the sign, they all said the same thing: Way Out.

God offers us similar signage. He is always faithful. He is always true. Thanks to the promise of 1 Corinthians 10:13, we might get tempted but we don't have to sin.

There's always a way out.

A SERIES OF SMALLER DOORS

What might the Way Out sign look like for you?

Well, the most effective way you can avoid sin is to not walk through the door marked Temptation in the first place. The main way out is to stay out. Don't go through the door. This means you build safeguards into the way you live, and these safeguards keep you far away from temptation. You don't stray anywhere near that doorway. Romans 13:14 invites you to "put on the Lord Jesus Christ, and make no provision for the flesh, to gratify its desires" (ESV). That's a verse you should have underlined in your Bible.

When you "make no provision for the flesh," it means you live wisely. You live with discretion. You err on the side of caution. You make environmental modifications—no matter how radical they might be. It's hard to do this alone, so you should be accountable to a few close friends and talk about real struggles and temptations with them.

THE MAIN WAY OUT IS TO STAY OUT.

_____

For example, maybe you don't have a problem with porn, but you see how porn could become a problem in your house. So in the spirit of living with discretion you install filters on all your family computers. Those filters help safeguard your integrity. You talk to your trusted friends about it, and they talk with you about what they're doing to place safeguards in their lives. That's smart. You took the way out—in this case, the way to stay out.

Suppose you do open that big door marked Temptation. You go through and find yourself heading toward sin. Watch closely. There are smaller doors marked Way Out all along the way.

Maybe your girlfriends invite you to go to Cancún. You sense a prompting from the Holy Spirit, and you think, *Hmm, last time I went to Cancún with my girlfriends, it was a disaster. I wiped out a good nine months of my spiritual progress.* So the way out for you is immediate and straightforward. You tell your girlfriends no, sorry, you're not going to be able to make it this time. That's how you make no provision for the flesh.

Or maybe you're a step through the doorway already. You're looking at pictures of sunshine and beaches and dreaming of fun in the sun in Cancún, even though you're aware it's not the smartest move for you. Mentally, you are straying further and further into the place of sin. You're inside the doorway. Fortunately, God is always faithful. So maybe when you go to book your ticket, your credit card gets declined. That's not the sign of a bad day. That's a Way Out sign. That's a work of the Holy Spirit. Take it.

Or maybe you go even further. You update your credit card info and book your plane ticket anyway, and now you and your girlfriends have flown to Cancún. Somebody suggests that you all go to the group's favorite club. You wince and feel the prodding of the Holy Spirit and think, *Okay, last time we went to that same club, and that's where all the trouble began.* You still have an out. You can say, "No, I'm not going to that club" or "No, let's go somewhere else" or "No, you guys go. I'm going to take a walk on the beach."

But now you're in the taxi headed to the club. You still sense the conviction of the Spirit—*Don't keep going.* By God's grace there's a tiny door by which you can escape.

"Hey, girls, I know this sounds like crazy town, but I'm getting out at the next intersection. I'm getting another taxi back to the hotel. No judgment intended and so sorry for the drama, but I need to go." Extreme, you say? Maybe. But resisting temptation is not a game. It's a war.

If you want a way out, God is faithful. The Holy Spirit will give you a way out, and the Holy Spirit will give you another out, and the Holy Spirit, in His mercy, will give you another out after that. The doorways might become smaller and smaller the further along you go. The way out is more difficult to take because you're further along the pathway, and the potential consequences if you opt not to take the way out become more serious.

But look closely: opportunities to take the way out are still there. The first doorway out is a regular-sized door you'd find in any house. The second doorway out is a pet-sized door that folks cut for Fido to get out. The third doorway out is a teeny-tiny Barbie house doorway that only your phone will slide through. But you can still win the battle. You don't have to give the Enemy a seat at your table. You can still get out!

The other main way to avoid sin is simply to stop gazing at the door marked Temptation. Go a different direction entirely. Exchange the door marked Temptation for the door marked Invitation. Focus on a different door, the door of Christ. Hebrews 12:1–2 says, "Let us throw off everything that hinders and the sin that so easily entangles. And let us run with perseverance the race marked out for us, *fixing our eyes on Jesus*, the pioneer and perfecter of faith" (italics added).

See, at its core, the gospel message is not "Don't sin." That message is often preached because it lands with lots of punch. *Don't sin! Don't sin! Don't sin!* But the message of the cross is far less about "Don't sin" and much more about "Come, walk with God." The gospel message is that through the work of Christ our sins are forgiven. We are new creations, and we can step into a relationship with Almighty God. Jesus offers us an abundant life that is life to the full (John 10:10). Paul, in 1 Thessalonians 3:8, said, "Now we really live."

Go back to Psalm 23 and John 10:1–18 and imagine life as a sheep with Jesus as your Good Shepherd. The point of those two passages is that God promises to guide you. Just as sheep can learn to recognize the voice of their shepherd, you are given the ability to hear the voice of Christ. You can see what the Shepherd is doing. You can rest in the Shepherd's care. You can move in step with the Shepherd. As you live closely with Jesus, you discover that you can trust God. You can look back on your life and see times He carried you, times He pulled you close, times He kept you out of danger, times He navigated you through. Intimacy with God is the way to true fulfillment. How do you keep the Enemy from sitting at your table? You keep your eyes on Christ.

Note again the story of Adam and Eve. Before the temptation came, there was an invitation for both of them to continue walking with God. Immediately after the fall, in Genesis 3:8, when Adam and Eve heard God "walking in the garden in the cool of the day," they recognized the sound because they were familiar with it. God had walked and talked with Adam earlier, when Adam named the animals. God had made Eve and "brought her to the man" (Genesis 2:22). They knew what it was like to walk with God. They were made in the image of God, and they knew what it was like to have a relationship with God and do God's work on earth—*with* God.

That was the larger gospel as Adam and Eve understood it. There was a definite command: *Don't sin. Don't eat of the fruit.* But there was larger good news that said, *Come and enjoy God.* That larger gospel is extended to you today. You're saved, yes.

But has God ever been more to you than a command not to sin? Is God larger to you than a ticket to heaven when you die? Sure, it's good you're saved. Sure, it's good you're forgiven. Sure, it's good you're going to heaven. Yet beyond that truth, God is greatly interested in you knowing Him, right now, today, long before you ever get to heaven. How well do you actually know God?

BABY ZEBRAS

When you're on the pathway to knowing God, it means you set your heart, purpose, and mind in that direction. When you begin to learn His Word, the Bible, you get to know Him and His character. When you walk with Him in continual prayer, you learn His ways. His words, ways, and character fulfill the needs in your life. Do you have a need for worth? For significance? For purpose? For love? For acceptance? For satisfaction? For peace? For the closest kind of companionship? For calm in the midst of a storm? Jesus fulfills those needs.

Those are the same needs the Enemy is exploiting. When you feel down, it's usually because needs of yours aren't being met. That's when the Enemy comes along and whispers, *If you want to feel better, then just go through this door marked Temptation. I'll give you a thrill. I'll give you a jolt of dopamine. I'll give you a rush of adrenaline.*

Nothing can satisfy your heart like God. Nothing keeps you from sin better than keeping your eyes on Christ. When you walk with God, you discover your true identity, worth, and purpose. That's where you discover you can trust God.

We looked at James 1:14, where "each person is tempted when they are dragged away by their own evil desire and enticed." James went on to describe a greater context: "Don't be deceived, my dear brothers and sisters. Every good and perfect gift is from above, coming down from the Father of the heavenly lights, who does not change like shifting shadows" (vv. 16–17).

Sin gives birth to death. Don't be deceived about that fact, James said. Going through the door marked Temptation leads only to sin and death. Nothing on the other side of that door is going to help you. Sin might feel good for a moment, but it's always less than God's best for you. Instead, go through the other door, the one marked Invitation. That's where you find every good and perfect gift. Those gifts come to you from Christ. What you're looking for is found through the other doorway. And the real reward isn't even about the gifts Jesus gives you. It's about walking through that doorway and getting God Himself.

Have you ever considered the tremendous benefits that exist for us on this side of Eden? Yes, we're living in a sin-stained and corrupted world. We're not in Paradise anymore. But we're also living with the knowledge of how far God Almighty will go for us. We're living with a knowledge of God's love that Adam and

Eve didn't have. When the serpent said to Eve, *Maybe God is holding out on you*, Eve had God's word at that point. She had what God had told her and Adam about Himself. She had a perfect environment to live in and enjoy. But she had little actual experience to back up God's promise.

We have experience. We have the death, burial, and resurrection of Christ in our story. We can point to the cross and say, "Actually, God's not holding out anything on us. That's what God's heart is like. God loved me so much He sent His Son to take away the sins of the world. That's a heart that scales any mountain. Kicks down any doors. Relentlessly pursues us down darkened alleyways. God will do anything to reach me with His love—including sending His only beloved Son to the cross and raising Him to life again. Thanks to Jesus, I am a new creation." Eve didn't know what we know. She did not know how far God would go. But we do.

A while back, I heard Priscilla Shirer talk about what zebras do with their young.[4] When a mama zebra gives birth, one of the first things she does is take her child away from the rest of the herd for a while. Why? Because the mother wants her child to learn to know her.

To the untrained eye, all zebras look the same. Even baby zebras have been known to mix up who their mom is. But every zebra has a unique pattern of markings on its head and face. When the mother zebra takes her baby away like that, the baby learns to identify exactly who its mother is. The child can see and hear the mother. It learns to recognize the mother's individual markings. For weeks and weeks, it's just mother and child, mother and child, mother and child.

Soon enough, the baby zebra is brought back to the herd. By then, the baby has learned a remarkable sort of discernment. It can see all these other animals that look and sound and smell almost the same and say, *No, not that one. No, not that one. No, not that one. Ah, that one—that's my mother.*

That level of familiarity and recognition is where God wants you to be with Him. God wants you to know Him without a doubt. All the Enemy does is lie. The Enemy wants to lead you astray so he can destroy you. But Jesus wants you to learn God's voice, to recognize God, to trust God. The quicksand has no more power. The door marked Temptation has no more appeal. You are set free. You can win the battle for your mind. You are invited to deeply and closely know God.

As part of that process, there's one more specific prayer that you can pray. When it comes to not giving the Enemy a seat at your table, this prayer—and all the freedom and invitation it brings—is perhaps the most powerful.

SEVEN

TAKE EVERY THOUGHT CAPTIVE

I'm a college dropout.

Not because I'm not smart enough. But because when I was eighteen years old I was losing the battle of my mind. The Enemy had gained a foothold in my life, and that foothold was called laziness. I could sleep through morning classes like a champ. If there had been an Olympic competition in skipping class and making excuses, I'd have gold medals hanging on the wall. Eventually, the letter arrived from the dean of my program requesting that I kindly take some time off from pursuing my university education.

No worries, I thought. *I'll enroll at the junior college in town.*

Not long after, I received a similar notice from them. I had succeeded in failing out of two schools in the same year.

Talk about the Enemy sitting at your table and eating your lunch!

All the while, I still had huge dreams. Through a powerful experience of being called to ministry, I knew God had big plans for my life. I could clearly see my future. But I had lost sight of what it was going to take to get there. I was pumped about eventually going to graduate school for further ministry training. I had just lost interest in the undergraduate grind necessary to get there.

Once the light bulb came on and I connected the two steps, I literally took the next exit on the freeway and within an hour was sitting in that same dean's office, begging him to let me back into Georgia State. He was gracious, and I was awakened to my future plans and what it was going to take to get there. My identity wasn't being a college strikeout. I was called by God to preach His Word. I had the capacity to sleep through class, for sure. But, as I demonstrated, I also had the ability to crush two years' worth of classes (crush in the very best way) in a little over a year. I graduated with my original freshman class and enrolled in grad school on schedule.

I won the battle of my mind. I woke up every day convinced God was going to accomplish through me all He had called me to do. I believed I could be who He created me to be.

Can you see where you want to be?

I'm not only talking about where you want to be in some personal accomplishment, business success, sports endeavor, or financial goal. I'm talking about where you want to be in your soul. I'm talking about being in charge of your thoughts, attitudes, and actions. I'm talking about moving into purpose and living the life God has designed you to live.

Perhaps the Enemy has convinced you that you can't move from where you are to where you want to be. You've listened to the voices of fear. You've been caught in the spiral of sin and temptation. You've convinced yourself you have no value. Your mind is clouded by worry and uncertainty. The Enemy has accomplished this by sitting down at your table, but you don't need to let him stay there and get comfortable. You do not have to entertain the Enemy's voice. Through Christ, you can move to a place of victory in your life.

This happens when you learn to win the battle for your mind. The Enemy knows this. One of his main ploys is to go after your thought life. He's patient too. In the garden of Eden, the serpent didn't shout his temptations to Eve over a loudspeaker. He planted seeds in her mind and waited. He prompted her to question God's goodness. He coaxed her to wonder if God was withholding something good from her. Eventually Eve relented and let those seeds take root. Eve acted out what she had been thinking about.

That's how the Enemy works. If he can win the battle for your mind, then he can win the battle for your life. In Numbers 13, when Moses dispatched the twelve spies to explore the land of

Canaan in preparation for Hebrew conquest, ten spies returned with a fearful, faithless report. "We can't attack those people," the ten spies said, shaking in their boots. "They are stronger than we are. . . . We seemed like grasshoppers in our own eyes, and we looked the same to them" (vv. 31, 33).

Hang on. How did the ten spies know what they looked like in the Canaanites' eyes? Did the spies ask their enemies, "Hey, what do you think of us? How small and puny do we look to you?" No, a seed had been planted in the spies' minds. They tended that seed and let it grow and acted on it, and as a result, they wandered in the desert for the next forty years. They never tasted the promises of God for their lives.

It didn't have to be that way, in the wilderness never tasting God's promises—not for them, and not for you and me today. Victory can be yours. Right here. Right now. Victory is about examining the seeds that have been scattered in your mind and not letting them take root. It's about pulling up and throwing away the thoughts that do not coincide with the heart of God. It's about changing the way you think. And one prayer helps in particular.

READINESS FOR THE POWER PRAYER

Maybe one of the seeds planted in your mind is doubt. You don't know if any of this teaching is going to work for you. You've tried other ways to change before, and none of them worked, so why should this? Or maybe some change will come, but it won't last because it's never lasted before.

Already the Enemy has influenced your mind. Seeds can be scattered in your mind anytime, anywhere, and particularly when you read a book such as this. Before the truth can set you free, you need to see the lies that are holding you hostage. Ask the Holy Spirit to reveal to you which lies you're believing. Ask Him to be specific. Are you having any of the following thoughts?

- *I'll never change.*
- *I'll feel better if I sin.*
- *The gospel doesn't really work.*
- *I'm not worth much.*
- *No one loves me.*
- *No one believes in me.*
- *I deserve to be bitter.*
- *I deserve to be filled with rage.*
- *I am my failure.*
- *I am my addiction.*
- *I'll always be this way.*

None of those thoughts came from God! Jesus Christ, the Good Shepherd of John 10 and Psalm 23, did not tell you that you're a failure. He doesn't prompt you to worry. He doesn't provoke you to fear. He provides clarity, not chaos. He doesn't stick your nose in the vomit of sin. He provides green pastures, not dry wastelands. If any of these things are in your life—fear, worry, temptation, feelings of worthlessness, feelings of confusion— guess what? The Enemy has shown up and dropped a seed in your thinking. He knows that if he can lodge a deceptive thought in your mind that goes unchecked, it will eventually take root and settle into your heart. If you harbor a deceptive thought and let it take up residence within you, in time, you will act on that thought.

Maybe you're saying, *What's the big deal? It's just a thought. Nobody sees it except me. It's harmless.* No. All the thoughts we entertain in our minds eventually get played out. Either our attitudes will reflect those deceptive thoughts or our behaviors will. "As he thinks in his heart, so is he" (Proverbs 23:7 NKJV). One way or another, those thoughts will harm us.

That's why it's so important, as we talked about in the last few chapters, for you to step into your new identity in Christ immediately. Jesus is already in the story of victory, and He has invited you into this story with Him. The way you step into that story is by reminding yourself of these truths:

- *I was a sinner saved by grace who is now a new creation. I do not have to sin.*
- *I am in Christ, and Christ is in me. Christ has all victory, and His victory is mine too.*

- *God is always faithful. He will always provide a way out. I can always take the way out.*

Stepping into these truths changes your mind. All twelve of the spies knew that the promised land was good. They all viewed the abundant milk and honey. They all saw a single grape cluster so big it took two men to carry it on a pole (Numbers 13:23). But ten of those spies didn't believe they could get to the promised land.

How about you? Do you believe you can live in victory? If the answer is no, the deceiver is winning the battle for your mind. He's real, and he has a real plan. He's circling your table, ready to sit. So keep this in mind: the stakes are high. This is *your life* we're talking about. This is your now. This is your future. This is your family. This is your sanity. Your peace. Your success. Your calling. Your destiny. This is everything God has made you to be. The Devil wants to destroy you. He has no mercy, and he has all the time in the world.

Fortunately, any seeds the Enemy scatters in your mind don't need to remain for more than a millisecond. Seeds do not need to take root. Any new seeds can be immediately removed. Even seeds that have been there for years can be removed. And it's not about you using your superpowers. I want to drive this point home. Victory is not about something you do. That's not the message here. The message is the gospel of Jesus Christ. It's about what Jesus does for you. Jesus won the total victory Himself. God makes the way.

So how do you live in victory?

THE WAR IS OVER; THE BATTLES ARE NOT

The word *victory* in the above verse is the Greek word *nikos*. It specifically connotes victory that has come about due to a conquest. In the New Testament, the word is always used to describe the conquest provided for the believer by Christ. He conquered all the powers of darkness and sin. Believers are in Christ, and Christ is in believers. The powers of darkness and the powers of sin cannot win the victory over any believer. The overall battle has been won. Jesus said on the cross, "It is finished" (John 19:30). In other words, "What I've come here to do is accomplished. You have been liberated. The victory is yours."

Picture the victory you own as if you were standing on the beaches of Normandy on D-Day Plus 1. Do you know what that means? D-Day was June 6, 1944, so D-Day Plus 1 is the term given to the day after D-Day—June 7, 1944.

D-Day was the largest amphibious invasion in military history.[1] More than 156,000 Allied troops stormed their way ashore on the Normandy coastline, pushing through a hail of Nazi machine-gun fire, grenades, and firepower. The Allies came in strong thanks to more than 6,900 ships and landing vessels, 2,300 aircrafts, 867 gliders, and 450,000 tons of ammunition. Casualties were heavy. Tragically, more than 4,400 Allied troops lost their lives on June 6. Yet by nightfall, the victory had been won. The five Normandy beaches—code-named Gold, Utah, Juno, Omaha, and Sword—were all secured. More troops began coming ashore. Temporary harbors were constructed. In time, the Allies would unload more than 2.5 million troops, 500,000 vehicles, and 4 million tons of supplies through the harbors at Normandy.

Historians agree that D-Day marked a decisive turning point in the war. Thanks to actions taken on D-Day, the outcome of World War II shifted significantly. The destiny of the entire world had changed. So imagine you're there on D-Day Plus 1. You're standing on one of the beaches on the day after the huge, bloody invasion. The overall war has been decided. Hitler's power has been broken. There's no way he can win now. From this beachhead of victory you can push forward and keep going. Why keep going? Well, even though the war in Europe is over, Hitler will still operate from a place of defeat for a while. He'll keep fighting even though he's been crushed.

In the next few weeks, many more skirmishes will come. You'll battle in the French town of Carentan. You'll capture the port of Cherbourg. You'll still need to liberate Paris on August 25. Some of the fighting will be intense. Over the next year, you'll still need to struggle in the fierce battle of Operation Market Garden. You'll hold the wintery line in the Battle of the Bulge. You'll still need to push your way into Nazi-occupied Germany and liberate the horrific concentration camps. On D-Day Plus 1, you'll need to get your mind around this truth: even though the war is over, some of your toughest fighting is still to come. Yet because the beachhead has been established, you will always fight from the place of overall victory.

In your spiritual life, Jesus gives you the *nikos*. He gives you His accomplished work on the cross, the defeat of sin. He has established a beachhead of victory so you can move forward. From this foundation of victory, you now fight. That's your mindset to prayerfully embrace today.

THE PRAYER OF POWER

Okay, it all leads up to this. The one huge prayer that holds the promise of winning the fight for your thoughts stems from this passage of Scripture:

> Though we live in the world, we do not wage war as the world does. The weapons we fight with are not the weapons of the world. On the contrary, they have divine power to demolish strongholds.

We demolish arguments and every pretension that sets itself up against the knowledge of God, and we take captive every thought to make it obedient to Christ. (2 Corinthians 10:3–5)

Let's unpack that. The weapons you fight with have divine power. Those weapons are outlined in Ephesians 6:1–18, the full armor of God: the righteousness we have from Christ, the full gospel of peace, faith, salvation, the Holy Spirit, the Word of God, and prayer. Those weapons have the power to demolish anything that sets itself up against God. With those weapons you don't need to let any harmful thought that floats through your mind settle down. In Christ, you do not need to let the Enemy sit at your table. How? The basis of the prayer is found right there in the text.

God, help me take captive every thought to make it obedient to Christ.

It sounds paradoxical, but it isn't. These two truths work together as one: Christ does all the work, yet you need to lean into that work by prayer and decisiveness. You must agree with Jesus.

In Christ, you have been given the opportunity because of the beachhead of victory to move forward, fighting in power. The power comes from Christ. The victory comes from Christ. Yet you must agree with Christ so you don't live in the double-barreled message of defeat. Nobody else is going to take your thoughts captive on your behalf. Nobody is going to climb into your head for you and get up into your thoughts and take captive everything that's coming against you. It's time for you to step up and take responsibility to partner with Christ in your destiny and your future and your victory.

Here's a hard truth, and I'm not going to shield you from this or attempt to candy-coat it: if you don't take a thought captive, the failure lies with you. I speak this truth in love to you in the same breath I preach it to myself. The failure is not because of your mother. It's not because of your stepdad. It's not because of any trouble that has come against you. If you are living in defeat, it's because you are allowing yourself to live in defeat. If you are losing the battle of your mind, it's because you are not willing to step up and say, "There's a fight to be fought, and I'm going to fight the battle to win my mind because I have the power of the finished work of Jesus."

So you must decide right now, today, to change the story of the battle for your mind. You do that by prayerfully taking every thought captive. How does that specifically work?

SEE THE LIE

First, you identify any deceptive thought in your mind. This sounds so basic, but it's amazing how many people do not do this. You must see that thought for what it is: a harmful lie. It's far too easy to coddle the thoughts that enter your mind. You are far too agreeable with your thought life. I know I am.

So a thought enters your mind. *Hey, it will feel better if I sin. If I overeat. If I run to lust. If I lash out in rage.* (Whatever your weak point is.) And you coddle that thought. You pamper it. You host it. You entertain it. You give it shelter and sustenance. You think, *You know, that's right. I will feel better if I sin. Life is super hard right now, so I deserve this. I felt horrible after I went to this familiar sin last time, and that's going to happen this time too. But I'm okay with feeling horrible in the long run if I can just feel better for a little while.* Boom. The Enemy has just sat down at your table.

Shout "No!" at this. Harmful thoughts must be identified for the lies they are. You have to examine that thought and say, "Hey, before you pitch a tent in my mind, let me take a good, hard look at you. Because when I look at you, I don't think you're congruent with the Word of God. And if you're not compatible with what God says, then God didn't send you my way. Get out!"

Here comes another thought into your mind: *Boy, am I pathetic.* Are you going to entertain that thought? Will you let it sit in your mind for a while? Or do you see it for what it is?

Ask yourself, *Where did that thought come from? Did it come from God? Does that thought line up with what God says in the Bible? Does my heavenly Father think I'm pathetic? No way. My heavenly Father is a Good Shepherd, and He leads me to green pastures. He restores my soul. He guides me in paths of righteousness for His name's sake. That doesn't sound like someone who'd call me pathetic. Oh yeah, and I remember that in Colossians 3:12*

I'm called "holy and dearly loved." So it's certainly not God who's calling me pathetic. If it's not God, I know right away this is the voice of the Enemy. I'm not going to entertain this thought. Get out!

NOT MY WILL BUT YOURS

So you've identified the thought as a lie. The next step is to bind that thought in Jesus' name. Look at the terminology in 2 Corinthians 10:5: "Take captive every thought to make it obedient to Christ." When you take something captive, you arrest it. You seize it by legal authority and put it into custody. You put handcuffs on it. You forcibly detain it. You take it captive so it will be stopped from hurting you or anybody else.

When thoughts are bound in Jesus' name, that's a prayer where you and Jesus agree that the Enemy has no place in your mind. You're saying, "God Almighty, I bind this thought in the name of Jesus Christ. I take captive this thought because You commanded me to. I'm using the power that's available to me because of the Holy Spirit, and with that power I'm choosing to live in agreement with You. This thought is taken captive. The thought holds no power over me. The thought is out of here. The thought is carted off to jail."

The prayers you make are to God. Yet sometimes I think it's good if Satan or his evil bunch actually hear our prayers. The spirit world is real and all around us, even though we don't see it. Scripture gives us no indication that Satan is omniscient. He doesn't know everything, everywhere, and at all times as God does. So I don't believe that Satan hears the thoughts in our minds. When I come against him in prayer, sometimes I'll want to speak the prayer out loud. I always do this in the tone of verse 9 of Jude. The archangel Michael was contending with the Devil and used these words: "The Lord rebuke you!" It means that I'm acknowledging that Jesus has the power and that Christ is in me.

Why do you specifically pray or rebuke Satan in Jesus' name? Because the power doesn't come from you. It comes from Jesus. Because you need to use the name of the One who has all power and authority (Matthew 28:18). Because all you do, "whether in word or deed, do it all in the name of the Lord Jesus" (Colossians 3:17).

Maybe at this point you're saying, *Oh, Louie's gone overboard. He's asking me to bind my thoughts in Jesus' name. Sure, I like Jesus, and I go to church, but this is starting to sound crazy.* Nope. What's crazy is agreeing with the Enemy that he can pitch a tent in your mind. What's crazy is you agreeing with sin. What's crazy is letting the Enemy sit down at your table. What's crazy is letting a murderer and deceiver influence you. Do not let the evil one win the battle for your mind!

When a questionable thought enters your mind, ask yourself if that thought lines up with the righteous character of God or what's stated plainly in Scripture. If it doesn't, bind that thought in the name of Jesus Christ. Speak that prayer out loud, or pray it in your mind to the Lord. Use this specific, deliberate prayer to prohibit that thought from taking root in your mind:

I bind this thought in Jesus' name!

Your goal, as 2 Corinthians 10:5 points out, is specifically to take the thought captive "to make it obedient to Christ." When a thought is obedient to Christ, it either aligns with Christ or is rejected by Christ and by God's teaching found in Scripture. See, if a thought is not taken captive by you in Jesus' name, that thought will take you captive. You will bind the thought, or the thought will, in time, bind you. So you better think quickly because something's getting bound. Use the name of Jesus with authority. Bind the thoughts that don't come from God and that don't match the Word of God.

Have you heard what happened with Jesus in the garden of Gethsemane on the night He was betrayed? Before Judas led the Roman troops up to Jesus and betrayed Him with a kiss, Jesus was praying in the garden. It was a time of great intensity and agony. Jesus' sweat fell in drops of blood to the ground. The night was so difficult, in fact, that Jesus prayed three times that God would not have Him go to the cross (Matthew 26:39, 42, 44).

In preparation for doing the greatest thing that's ever been done on planet Earth, Jesus was going through the greatest

USE THE NAME
OF JESUS WITH
AUTHORITY.
BIND THE
THOUGHTS
THAT DON'T
COME FROM
GOD AND THAT
DON'T MATCH
THE WORD
OF GOD.

testing first. (As a sidelight—if you want to do something great for God, then get ready to be tested greatly first. You'll be tested greatly so you can be trusted greatly.)

Ultimately, Jesus surrendered His own struggle with taking on our sin to the Father's desire to make us holy. Even Jesus took captive His thoughts and made them obedient to God Almighty. Jesus ended His prayers by saying, "Not my will, but yours" (Luke 22:42). Even in this strongest of temptations, Jesus did not sin. This is the perfect model of taking thoughts captive! The pattern was set by Jesus Himself.

DJ OF YOUR THOUGHTS

Okay, first you identified the harmful thought. Second, you took that thought captive in Jesus' name. Now, third, you change the narrative of your story with Scripture. When times of troubles come and you want to jump into sin, this is how you change the trajectory of your story. You do this, primarily, by knowing Scripture.

Yep, you memorize Scripture and then replay Scripture in your mind. You exchange the deceptive thoughts for thoughts of truth. You familiarize yourself with what the Bible says and then repeat God's truth to yourself again and again so you know without a doubt what the truth is, and so you can stay on the path of truth.

"But Louie," people say. "I don't have time to memorize

Scripture." Really? You have time for a workout. You have time to read three new business proposals before work tomorrow. You have time to binge-watch a TV series over a weekend. You have time to listen to a podcast in your car during your morning commute. You have time to entertain harmful thoughts in your mind. So you have time to memorize Scripture. If you want victory, you have to be ready to fight. If you're not ready to fight, you're not going to win. Once you lose the battle for your mind, you are done. Defeated.

Start winning the battle for your mind by writing out God's truth on index cards and putting them on the tray on the exercise bike. Each morning at the gym, study Scripture on those cards for half an hour. Or cut out one TV show every other night and use that time to memorize Scripture instead. Or download an audible version of Scripture and listen to it in your car during your morning commute, choosing to fill your mind with God's truth, over and over again. You can start winning the battle of your mind right now. Renew your mind to the truth. Set your mind on that truth. Remind yourself often, and watch God set you free.

Have you ever considered all the Bible verses that instruct you and me to place Scripture firmly in our minds? Let me paraphrase just a few. Psalm 119:11 tells you to store up God's Word in your heart so that you might not sin. Joshua 1:8 tells you never to let God's Word depart from you. You're to meditate on it all the time. Colossians 3:16 tells you to let God's Word dwell in you richly. Matthew 4:4 says you're to live by God's Word like it's food for your life. Hebrews 4:12 describes God's Word as living and active. John 15:7 says you're to let God's Word abide in you. Deuteronomy 11:18–20 encourages you to put Scripture into your heart and mind, writing it on hands and foreheads, teaching it to your children, talking about it at home and when you're away, thinking through Scripture when you lie down and get up. Psalm 19:7 says that you're to dwell on Scripture because it helps restore your soul. Psalm 119:32 encourages you to run in the pathways of God's commands—for He sets your heart free.

When Jesus was tempted in the wilderness, how did He refute the Enemy? By quoting Scripture back to the evil one. "It is written . . . it is written . . . it is written." That's the winning tactic for us as well. Scripture needs to be wrapped throughout your life. It needs to be before your eyes and in your ears and all through your mind. It needs to be in your home and in your locker and on your computer and on your mirror and at your desk. It needs to be talked about and sung about and permeating the music you listen to. Scripture can keep you from sinning (Psalm 119:11). It can help you overcome worry (Philippians 4:6). It establishes your faith and helps you mature in the Lord (Colossians 2:6–7). It helps you discover God's good and perfect will for your life (Romans 12:2). When you fill your mind with Scripture, you get to control the playlist of your mind.

You become the DJ of your own thoughts.

FREEDOM OR LEEKS?

Finally, the Bible indicates that you can play offense with your thought life. It's so easy to slip. It happens all the time. You start identifying harmful thoughts, binding them in Jesus' name, and memorizing Scripture, but you're tempted to return to your former way of life. The past always looks better in hindsight than it actually was when you were living through it the first time. *Oh, man, remember how I used to retreat into that fantasy? Remember how I used to escape to that way of thinking?*

After the children of Israel were released from bondage in Egypt, they actually dreamed of returning. Numbers 11:5–6 records how they sat around complaining about manna, the perfect food that God had provided for them in the wilderness. Instead of going forward in victory, they remembered with fondness the "cucumbers, melons, leeks, onions and garlic" of Egypt. How crazy was that?! The Israelites must have really liked onions. They liked onions so much they were willing to trade their freedom for onions. *Oh sure, let's just go back to Egypt and become slaves again so we can eat onions.*

Philippians 4:8 offers a different route for us. It doesn't give us a step-by-step guide so much as a compass. It doesn't tell us specifically what to think, but it does offer various categories to think about. That's how to play offense. Instead of playing defense with the harmful thoughts that come your way, you take action and deliberately place helpful thoughts into your mind. Here are the categories to think about as found in Philippians 4:8.

Whatever is . . .
> true
>
> noble
>
> right
>
> pure
>
> lovely
>
> admirable
>
> excellent
>
> praiseworthy

Think about these things. Memorize Philippians 4:8, and then think through each category as outlined in that verse. Ask yourself, *What are truthful things I can think about right now? What are noble things?* And so on. Go all the way through the verse. Maybe the thoughts that come into your mind will be linked to specific verses. Or maybe the thoughts simply will honor God. You'll think of how much you love your family. You'll think of how much you enjoy skateboarding. You'll imagine a perfect sunrise. Or being on a hike with your friends.

Here's one great way to change your narrative: go on the offensive by thinking about these things first thing each morning. Carry them with you through each day. Don't stop telling yourself these truths until you fall asleep at night. Or another approach is to think about one category each day, all day. One for each day of the week. Imagine the results if you concentrate on thinking about *admirable* things for a whole day. Or grab hold of a specific scriptural truth for the day, such as these:

- **Monday.** My God knows my name. (Isaiah 43:1)
- **Tuesday.** My God goes before me. (Deuteronomy 31:8)
- **Wednesday.** I can do all things through Christ who strengthens me. (Philippians 4:13)
- **Thursday.** My present suffering pales in comparison to my future glory. (Romans 8:18)
- **Friday.** No weapon formed against me will prosper. (Isaiah 54:17)
- **Saturday.** I am a child of God. (Romans 8:16)
- **Sunday.** The same power that raised Jesus from the dead lives in me. (Ephesians 1:18–20)

I practice this myself. Early this morning as I was working on this chapter, the thought suddenly was in the forefront of my mind that maybe this book wouldn't help anybody after all. Maybe I was just pounding away at the keyboard for nothing. *Will anyone want to read this? Will anyone care?* All this negativity started clouding my mind. I sat in those thoughts for a few moments and felt myself growing depressed. Then I realized what was happening. Out loud in my study I said, "Lord, I need help. I know this is not from You."

I specifically prayed, taking those thoughts captive in Jesus' name.

Then I went on offense. What were the true and noble and right and good things I could think of? I started thinking of people who could be freed in Jesus' name from harmful thoughts. I thought about people who would choose not to let the Enemy sit at their table. Then a verse from my daily Bible reading returned to my mind—Joshua 1:5: "As I was with Moses, so I will be with you." Like a bombshell, that truth dislodged the negative thoughts that were attempting to set up shop in my mind.

That Scripture verse became my new narrative for the rest of the day. I reminded myself of that verse as I returned to work. The same God who was with Moses is the God who is with me.

And the Enemy did not sit at my table.

But what if the Enemy had sat down? I don't want to undermine the biblical teaching in this chapter in any way by offering a quick caveat. Yet I do want to acknowledge the reality of Hebrews 12:1–2, that there are sins that *so easily* entangle us. If you sin, are you immediately sunk? If you let the seed of a thought take root in your mind, if you let the Enemy sit at your table, is there still hope? Yes, great hope—because of God's abundant grace.

EIGHT

GRACE THAT SILENCES SHAME

After all your prayerful, grace-fueled efforts to turn the Enemy away, what happens if you give him a seat at your table anyway? Is God finished with you, or are you disqualified from having a relationship with God or from serving Him? The simple answer is no. The essence of the gospel is that God forgives sins through Jesus Christ and makes you brand new. The requirement for you is confession, admitting to the Lord that you have been entertaining the Enemy's thoughts or acting on those thoughts. When you repent, God wipes out your sins. God forgives you and cleanses you. God ejects the Devil from your table. Proverbs 28:13 points to the strength of confession: "Whoever conceals their sins does not prosper, but the one who confesses and renounces them finds mercy."

Yet even after we confess, two outcomes of sin often remain: guilt and shame. Often they get lumped together, but they're actually different. Sometimes people use those words and concepts interchangeably, but it's important to see the distinction.

Guilt is the position of being accountable for sins and shortcomings. It's a legal term that points to remorse. Within a framework of spiritual justice, you must take responsibility for choices you make when those choices fall short of God's standard. You have done or thought or said something improper, dishonorable, false, ignoble, reprehensible, impure, or unlovely. You've given the Enemy a seat at your table. The gavel comes down. The verdict comes in. By your actions or attitudes of the heart, you have fallen short of the glory of God, and you are responsible for it. You are guilty.

Shame, on the other hand, is the feeling of being defined by your sin and shortcomings. Shame acknowledges guilt, yet it intertwines the sin with your identity. Whereas guilt is a legal and spiritual state, shame is an emotional and mental state. When you experience guilt, you admit that you did something wrong. You say, "I have done something wrong" or "I have thought or said something bad." Yet when you experience shame, you take the sin upon yourself. You say, "I am something wrong" or "I am bad."

I want to address both guilt and shame because they are separate—even though they have the same solution. The pathway to freedom from both guilt and shame is the story of grace. Certainly in a legal and social framework there may need to be restitution made or apologies given or time served or fines paid or justice restored—and these can be part of the solution, sure. Yet the ultimate solution is always the grace of God. Many of us walk around carrying the weight of guilt and shame. These prevent us from walking in the freedom that was purchased for us at the cross. It doesn't need to be this way. We can have victory.

THE GRIT OF GRACE

The pathway to freedom is open to all people in the covering of grace. Grace isn't some ethereal, flimsy, milquetoast kind of thing. Grace has grit, backbone, and muscle. Grace is the left hook that destroys the power of sin.

So let's first see how grace destroys shame. Shame is a powerfully destructive force. It causes you to feel as if you're unworthy of God's love, acceptance, purposes, or plans. Shame causes us to feel marred so strongly that we feel damaged beyond repair. When you feel shame, you're prone to hide. You try to hide from God behind denial or by trying to keep out of His way. Or you hide from people behind layers, walls, titles, busyness, or accomplishments.

You don't want anybody to know you, so you keep people away at arm's length. Or you don't want anybody to know what happened to you. Shame imprisons you and me to the past.

How very telling that when God created Adam and Eve in the garden of Eden, the Bible says that "Adam and his wife were both naked, and they felt no shame" (Genesis 2:25). Before the fall, everything God created was described as "good," and being naked and unashamed was part of the goodness of Paradise. Yes, the garden was beautiful. Yes, there were plants and food and animals. Everything was in pristine condition. And note that the ultimate description of goodness in Paradise was a lack of shame.

Then came the fall. Adam and Eve made disastrous decisions that resulted in huge consequences. Earth broke apart as a result of their choices. Both guilt and shame entered into their story—and into ours too. One minute Adam and Eve were naked and unashamed; the next minute they were hiding from God, desperately trying to cover themselves with fig leaves.

Fortunately, even back in the garden, God formed a rescue plan. With Adam and Eve, God sheltered and clothed the two humans in garments of animal skin that He made for them. God pointed to the future and to the cross, when the serpent would harm Jesus by striking His heel, but Jesus would gain full victory by crushing the serpent's head (Genesis 3:15). In other words, God would destroy sin and death and fully reconnect people to the purposes and personhood of God.

Thanks to the work of Jesus on the cross, you and I can live free from shame. Don't let that truth pass you by. Shame does not need to be part of your story! We'll talk more about this in a little bit.

JESUS SETS YOU FREE

Second, let's look at how grace is also the solution to guilt. The grace of God moves into your story, and through the work of Jesus on the cross, the grace of God cancels your spiritual guilt and sets you free. Grace positions you rightly before God. There is a penalty to be paid for wrongdoings, yet Jesus already took the penalty of sin for you. Jesus has set you free.

We see hints of the grace you and I enjoy today even in the Old Testament. God was continually patient with His people, constantly waiting for them to respond to His holiness. Isaiah 6 records the prophet Isaiah seeing a vision of the Lord and heaven. It was a beautiful and powerful vision, and when he saw this vision, Isaiah didn't say, "Oh wow, that's cool." He was guilt stricken. He cried, "Woe to me! . . . I am ruined! For I am a man of unclean lips, and I live among a people of unclean lips, and my eyes have seen the King, the LORD Almighty" (v. 5). Isaiah felt completely shattered before God. Isaiah saw God and instantly saw the gap between who he was and who God is.

Isaiah's response points us to the finished work of Jesus on the cross. You can step into that finished work by the act of repentance, when you say the equivalent of Isaiah's words: "Woe is me. I've fallen short of God's holy standard. I've fallen short of what God intended. I've fallen short of God's best for my life. I admit it. I take responsibility for it. I realize that I am accountable for my choices and my sin before Almighty God." This is simply true—I am accountable for my sin—whether or not I admit it or respond emotionally.

Repentance is not a negative thing. Your act of admitting guilt opens a doorway called grace, and God comes to you through that doorway and does for you what none of us can do for ourselves. Grace is what was extended to Isaiah. The great news is that verses 6 and 7 tell of an angel who flew to Isaiah with a burning coal in his hand. Imagine yourself in Isaiah's shoes. He saw a seraph, an amazing six-winged celestial being, rushing at him through the air. The angel was carrying a blazing coal from the altar of God. I bet Isaiah assumed it was all over; he was finished. Isaiah expected to be exterminated. Instead, the angel touched Isaiah's mouth and said, "See, this has touched your lips; your guilt is taken away and your sin atoned for" (v. 7). That was great news for Isaiah because it meant he wasn't wiped out. Isaiah's repentance opened the doorway of grace. God came through that doorway and in essence said, "No, I'm not going to exterminate you. I'm going to exterminate your guilt. Your guilt is taken away. Your sin is atoned for."

When we fast-forward the story to the New Testament, we see another live burning coal has come down from heaven, the Holy One of God, Jesus Christ. He gave His innocent life and took on our guilt on Calvary's hill. Through His death, burial, and resurrection, Jesus rang the bell of our freedom. Jesus was pure and innocent, and on the cross a great exchange took place in heaven's courthouse. You and I were guilty of our sins and shortcomings, but God took our guilt and placed it instead on His innocent and righteous and willing Son. Then God took the innocence and righteousness of His Son and made it available to us. To everyone who repents, God proclaims forgiveness in the same way that the seraph said to Isaiah, "Your guilt is taken away. Your sin is atoned for." Through Christ, you are innocent. You are righteous. You are set free by a holy and righteous God. All your guilt was taken by Jesus. You are made brand new.

This is stated clearly in 1 John 1:9. The apostle was addressing new believers, helping them understand the power of the gospel, and he wrote, "If we confess our sins, he is faithful and just and will forgive us our sins and purify us from all unrighteousness." That means that the action of your confession is vitally important. When you confess, you admit that you are responsible for the sin in your life. You are saying, "I did it, and it was wrong." But here's the biggest news of all: if you do sin as a Christian, you confess your sin to clear the air in your fellowship with God. Because of the cross you are already forgiven. Jesus isn't going back to the cross and dying again. His forgiveness work is finished. So you say, "Father, I'm so sorry I sinned. I confess it. Thank You that in Christ I am forgiven. I receive it and want You to give me the grace and power to walk in a different direction." You confess both your sin and His forgiveness. That's great news, a real reason to celebrate!

Yet the Enemy will not go quietly on this one. He'll do all he can to keep you on a guilt trip indefinitely. Do you recognize his voice of dread? *Well now, I see that you're a Christian. I see that you believe you're going to heaven when you die. Well, that's just great. But I'm going to make sure your life feels like hell right now by pointing out to you everything wrong you've ever done, everything wrong you're doing right now, and everything wrong you're going to do in the future. That's right—I'm booking your tickets for a one-way cruise. You're going on a guilt trip, and I'm the captain of that ship, mister.*

It's far too easy to jump on that cruise. The Enemy remembers everything, and he'll bring all the ugly details back to life. He'll work hard to convince you that if you keep your sins hidden, all will be well. If you just press those sins down hard enough, or maybe if you just party it up hard enough—that's what is needed to feel good.

No. That never works. Time to jump ship. Your guilt is never removed when you hide. It's only when you bring your guilt into the spotlight of Christ's grace that your sins are atoned for and your guilt is removed. In Jesus' holy, loving, and kind presence, you can say, "Lord, I confess that I've done some wrong things. I also want to let You know that some wrong things have been done to me. These things have made me feel marred. Damaged. Hurt. I've been both a perpetrator of sin and a victim of sin. But I want Your forgiveness and Your freedom. I don't want to hide from You. I want Your eyes to see all that I've done and all that's been done to me. By Your work, the effects of sin are cancelled. By Your stripes I am healed."

THE REDEFINED YOU

Grace not only cancels guilt and shame but also redefines you and me. The biggest change in definition is from "failure" to "family."

Nathaniel Hawthorne wrote a book in 1850 called *The Scarlet Letter*. In the story, a young woman named Hester Prynne has a baby through an affair. Hester is jailed for adultery, made to feel like a failure. When the baby is about three months old, Hester is released from jail, her initial debt to society paid. Yet in order to shame her permanently, the townspeople make Hester stand on a scaffold in the town square for three hours wearing a red cloth *A* stitched onto the front of her dress. The legacy of the public shaming will be her ongoing punishment. For years afterward, Hester is treated as an outcast. She is defined by what she has done.

Many of you are walking around with a scarlet letter of your own. You are defined by your sin. You look at that letter on your chest and say, "Yep, that's me." Or maybe it was somebody else's sin that got exported into your life. Even then, you look in the mirror and say, "I am damaged. I am ruined." You take other people's failures and wear them as your own.

God changes your identity. The Enemy wants to define you by your scars. Jesus wants to define you by His scars. The grace of Jesus Christ removes your old identity and replaces it with a brand-new identity. First John 3:1 says, "See what great love the Father has lavished on us, that we should be called children of God. *And that is what we are!*" (italics added). That is your new identity. You are a son or daughter of God. You are a child of the King. You are written into God's will, and you are an heir of everything God has. You are a beneficiary of the lavish love of God, which has changed you from failure to family. Grace not only cancels guilt and shame; grace redefines you. You are a beloved family member of God, and because of that you are given a seat at the table with Almighty God.

Consider the life of the apostle Peter, and how God changed him from a failure into family. A bit of backstory will help. Did you know his name wasn't even Peter at first? His original name was Simon, but when Jesus first met him, Jesus gave him the

THE ENEMY
WANTS TO
DEFINE YOU
BY YOUR
SCARS.
JESUS
WANTS TO
DEFINE
YOU BY HIS
SCARS.

---

name Peter. Peter tended to act first and think second. So when Jesus met this rough-and-tumble fisherman, Jesus nicknamed him "the Rock." Peter's bold personality came out in many places throughout the Gospels.

On the night of the Last Supper, Jesus threw a dinner party for His twelve closest followers. It was revealed that someone was going to betray Him that night. The disciples couldn't believe it. Particularly Peter. He was especially vocal, full of indignation and well-meaning boasting. *Not me!* he said. *Maybe some of those other guys will flake out, but not me. I'll never betray You. I'll never bail. You can count on me, Jesus. I love You more than all these guys. I'm ready to go with You to prison and to death.*

Jesus looked at him and said, "Peter, before the rooster crows today, you will deny three times that you know me" (Luke 22:34).

The Last Supper concluded. The disciples went to the garden of Gethsemane where Jesus prayed in great earnest. Judas led the Roman soldiers to Jesus, and in the dim torchlight Judas betrayed Jesus with a kiss. Jesus was arrested. For the rest of the night Jesus was shuttled back and forth between various government entities in Jerusalem. Jesus was mocked, scorned, questioned, spit on, and beaten. We don't know where all the rest of the disciples were, yet we know that Peter followed at a distance. At least his good intentions got him that far. But then came Peter's crunch time.

Far into that unholy night, Jesus was being questioned at the home of the high priest, Caiaphas. The night was cold, and

Peter stood outside in the courtyard warming his hands by a fire. A number of folks were standing around, and a young woman began to question Peter. She recognized him as being one of Jesus' followers, but Peter said no, she must have been mistaken. Someone else recognized Peter as being one of Jesus' followers too, but again Peter denied it. About an hour later, another person recognized Peter as a Galilean and asked if he knew Jesus. This was Peter's moment. The full pressure was on. He was afraid. By that time of the night, he must have been hungry, lonely, tired, and fearful. Yet a third time, Peter denied knowing Him.

Let's stop for a moment, because isn't that the essence of sin right there? You and I get into those times and places where we are pressured. We feel hungry, lonely, tired, fearful, or angry, and we face the opportunity to take a step toward Jesus or a step away from Jesus. In those times of pressure, it's easy for us to say, "I don't know Jesus. I don't want anything to do with Him. No, I'm not following Jesus right now." But it's far better for us to run toward Jesus and refuse the Enemy a seat at our table.

With Peter's third denial, the rooster crowed. Peter realized what he had done. He'd sinned mightily. He had sounded so strong in his love for Christ during the Last Supper, yet when the pressure was on in the courtyard of Caiaphas, Peter had crumbled. He knew this. The Bible says he was remorseful and wept bitterly (Luke 22:62). The story continued, and Jesus went to the cross as scheduled. (As a side note, can we just celebrate the fact that even if we deny Jesus, God still moves on with His plans? Even if we're faithless, God is still faithful.) Peter might have bailed on the mission, but Jesus didn't.

So the death and burial of Jesus took place. Early on Sunday morning, two women went to the tomb, but the tomb was empty. The women hurried back and described the scene to the rest of the disciples. Peter ran straightaway to the tomb. He saw the strips of burial cloth lying by themselves and tried to make sense of it. Eventually Jesus appeared to the disciples several times, but Peter and Jesus didn't interact much during those first few times, at least not that we're aware of. Then we fast-forward to the encounter recorded in John 21, and all the cards are laid on the table.

The story unfolded in Galilee. Peter and six of the disciples had gone fishing. They had fished all night but hadn't caught anything—and then Jesus showed up. Incidentally, some scholars think it's no big deal that Peter and the disciples had returned to fishing. The guys had bills to pay. They had to get on with their lives. But I see the act of returning to fishing as a negative. Why? Because think back to what you know of Peter's original commission three years earlier. "Follow Me," Jesus had said then, "and I will make you fishers of men" (Matthew 4:19 NKJV). In other words: "Follow Me because I have a plan and a purpose for your lives." But now Peter had returned to his old job, to his former way of living. He'd ignored his new commission. He'd gone fishing for *fish* again. I think Peter knew he was wearing the identity of "three-time betrayer" on his chest, and he didn't believe a three-time betrayer had any place in the plans and purposes of Jesus anymore.

Ever been in a similar place? You've denied Jesus, so now you feel cloaked in shame. Or you've ignored Jesus, or overlooked Jesus, or forgotten Jesus, and now you're back to your old way of life. You've sinned, you've given the Enemy a seat at your table, so now you're hiding from God. When that happens, you go to a familiar place, even though the familiar place isn't part of Jesus' call on your life. You go to a place you know, and know all too well. You go to the place that's easy to go to but seldom beneficial. It might not be a place of debauchery and gross sin, but merely a place where you think you can do life without God—perhaps the grossest sin of all.

In a place like this, it's hard to believe you can ever be restored.

THE RESTORED YOU

Back to Peter's story. Just as day was breaking, Jesus stood on the shore. He addressed the disciples in the boat familiarly, asking if they'd caught any fish (John 21:4–5). Jesus already knew the answer. In the English language we miss the nuance. When Jesus called to the disciples in the boat, His statement implied a negative response. Translated more literally, Jesus said something more like this: "Guys, have you caught anything? *No, I see you haven't.*" In today's vernacular, Jesus was saying, "How's that working for you?" In other words, you've been out all night and it's been a long night of nothing. *How's that working for you?* You've forgotten your original commission. *How's that working for you?* You've returned to a familiar, convenient place, but I have so much more for you than this familiar, convenient place. *How's that working for you?*

That's why this next bit of advice is so powerful. Jesus told the disciples to throw their nets on the other side of the boat. Don't you think they'd tried that already? They'd been out all night. They were experienced fishermen. They must have tried the front of the boat, the back of the boat, the right side, the left side. They'd tried everything. So why was it so different when Jesus told them to throw their nets on the other side of the boat?

The difference was because Jesus was behind the declaration. Peter and the disciples were given the opportunity to follow Jesus' voice. It was as if Jesus was saying to them, and particularly to Peter, "Follow Me. Even now. Even here. Even when you've gone back to your old ways." Isaiah 30:21 extends a similar call: "Whether you turn to the right or to the left, your ears will hear a voice behind you, saying, 'This is the way; walk in it.'" That's the voice of God. Are you listening?

Fortunately, Peter and the disciples followed Jesus' voice, and their nets instantly became full. They were about a hundred yards from shore. Peter got so excited that he jumped into the sea and swam to land to see for himself that it really was Jesus. The other disciples followed in the boat, dragging the full nets. When they got to the shore, they saw a charcoal fire and fresh bread. Jesus welcomed the disciples to join Him for breakfast with some of the fish they'd just caught. I love that this was Jesus' invitation to the guys, including Peter. Jesus wasn't there to interrogate Peter. Jesus simply invited Peter to breakfast on the beach.

How does Jesus restore you and me after we fall? The way Jesus responded to Peter is key for us today. Peter had denied Jesus during a time of Jesus' great need, and now Jesus had every right to shame him. To identify him by his sin. Nobody would have been surprised if Jesus had said something like this: "Hey, Peter! I heard that you denied Me three times. Are you for real? I hate to be a told-you-so, but I told you so. Why did you let Me down at the most critical moment of My mission? Are you even sorry? You're worthless, Peter. Useless. You're a hypocrite. Get out of here!" No, He didn't say anything like that to Peter, and He doesn't say anything like that to you and me. He simply said to Peter, "Come and have breakfast" (John 21:12). In other words: "Come close to Me. I bet you're hungry. Here's some warm baked bread. Here's barbecued fish fresh off the grill. I bet you're tired, cold, and wet. Come by this warm fire. Sit and rest awhile and dry your damp clothes."

What do you think Jesus will say to you when He takes you for breakfast? Often we adopt the voice of the accuser in our own lives. We absolutely should call sin what it is, to recognize sin as far short of God's best for our lives. But after we sin we add on words of accusation and heap them on ourselves. We tell ourselves we're done for. Useless. Finished. Or we imagine Jesus saying those things to us. Yet Romans 8:1 says, "There is now no condemnation for those who are in Christ Jesus." Jesus gave us such a perfect picture of that verse in His dealings with Peter. Jesus offers us similar kindness.

After the meal, Jesus had some more kind words for Peter. Sometimes we imagine Jesus and Peter walking down the beach by themselves so they could have a private conversation, but John recorded those next words, so he must have been within earshot. I believe this conversation took place around the campfire, with all the rest of the guys there. Jesus asked one question three different ways. Essentially, He wanted to know, "Peter, do you love Me? Do you love Me more than these boats and nets and fish and these things that you'd given your life to but that I'd called you away from?"

When Peter affirmed his love for the Lord, Jesus replied, "Feed my sheep" (John 21:17).

Right there, Jesus did more for Peter—and more for us—than we can imagine. Jesus was telling Peter that he wasn't finished. Peter was going to be the rock on which the mission of God would be established and carried forward. Jesus was telling Peter that his identity wasn't going to be a denier of Jesus. He was going to be a hero of the faith and a legend in the church. In fact, Peter would one day very soon preach the gospel in the power of the Holy Spirit, and three thousand people would be saved that day (Acts 2:14–42).

Sure, there were consequences to Peter's denial of Jesus. Two thousand years later, we're still studying the story. Peter's denial didn't get swept under the rug or erased from the memory bank of humanity. There were consequences for Peter, just like there are consequences to your decisions and my decisions too.

Yet Jesus never focused on the failure. He focused on the restoration. Grace removed Peter's guilt, and grace also removed Peter's shame. Peter's identity was no longer wrapped up in the denial. Peter failed, but he wasn't a failure. He wasn't useless. Peter's life was no longer marked by shame. Grace redefined Peter as a friend and family member of God Almighty.

That's what the grace of God does for you and me too.

THE RADIANT YOU

It's so easy to feel the effects of guilt and shame, to wallow around in them for a long time, even for a lifetime. Whenever we wallow in guilt and shame over our sins, we are stamping ourselves "damaged goods." Or if something bad happened to us and we're affected by sins of others, it's easy to walk around with the labels of "abused" or "hurt" or "harmed." But that is not who you are. Jesus says, *No, that is not your identity. Sin is what was done to you, or sometimes it's what you did, but sin is not who you are. You are family. You are a daughter of Almighty God, or a son of Almighty God. You are an heir to the King of the universe. That's who you truly are.*

When Jesus invites you to breakfast on the beach, He simply asks you if you love Him. If your answer is yes, Jesus proceeds with the restoration. He says, *That's great. My grace covers your guilt. My grace changes your shame. I want you to become a leader in My church. I want you to feed My sheep. I want you to be a part of My mission. I want you to love God and love other people in My name. You do not have to sit in the back row for the rest of your life. You do not have to live in the shadows. You don't have to build protective walls around yourself. You don't have to hide from the people who love you and care for you. They'll help love you and restore your integrity, and your call is to help take My name to the world, and I want you in the front row on that mission. You are My chosen instrument to carry forth the plans and purposes of God. You are not going to live defined by shame or guilt. You are going to live defined by Me. Since you love Me, let's not go backward. Let's go forward, together.*

The Enemy wants to twist that. He wants to keep sitting at

your table, chatting it up with you. The Enemy wants you listening to his voice. The Enemy wants you losing the battle for your mind. The Enemy wants you looking away from the Lord. But Psalm 34:5 points you in a different direction: "Those who look to him [the Lord] are radiant; their faces are never covered with shame." Do you think of yourself as "radiant"? That's a powerful image and the opposite of shame. If you're looking to the Lord, you are radiant. Your face is reflecting the light and love of Christ. You are never covered with shame.

It can be hard to forgive yourself. I get it. Yet your new identity doesn't spring from *you* letting yourself off the hook. Your new identity springs from the realization that Jesus forgives you. Jesus lets you off the hook. Your new identity forms when you agree with Jesus. He says you're a son or daughter of God. Jesus says you're forgiven. Do you agree with Him?

If Jesus says you can go forward, you can go forward.

STAGGERED BY THE MOUNTAIN

Often at sporting events, the home organization arranges a promotion for fans in the stadium that involves randomly selecting a couple of people sitting in the "nosebleed" section and moving them to the front row. You see the couple on the video screen losing their minds with excitement as an usher arrives to escort them from the cheap seats to ones that are up close to the action. From crummy to club level. Everyone wants the best seat.

This brings us to the most perplexing concept in Psalm 23, one we've touched on already, but one I want to explore in much more depth. Really, this is the crux of the book. Why did God set the table for you *in the presence* of your enemies? Why do they get ringside seats at your table?

Wouldn't it make more sense if the table was simply in His presence? Why not vanquish the foes? Change the circumstances? Get rid of the cancer? Bring back your loved one? Shut down the voices spreading the lies?

To uncover the answer, picture the table again. You have been invited to a feast. The table is covered with all the things that satisfy and sustain you. Yet you're not primarily interested in the size of the strawberries or the steak that's grilled perfectly to your liking. You've started to realize that the power of this table is not what's on it, but who's at it. You are sitting with the King. Not just some run-of-the-mill earthly king. You are dining with the King of the ages. The God of the cosmos. You're at the table with the wisest, kindest, most loving, most creative, most joy-filled, most interesting person in the universe.

In the midst of the battles that are raging, He is near. The Good Shepherd is available and accessible. He has invited you to go as deep in your relationship with Him as you desire. Let that sink in for a moment; the King of the universe wants to spend one-on-one time with . . . you.

Shelley and I have a goldendoodle named London. To know this dog is to love her. She's awesome and gets a lot of airtime in our world. She's chill and has a knack for making people feel good. She also has a knack for snacks. Whenever we take her out for a walk, strangers stop us on the street and ask to say hello and pet her. They don't say hello to us. They just want to ask about our dog.

London's name is special to us, too, because she's named after a city Shelley and I absolutely love. We first traveled to London in 1988 and have been back a number of times over the years—sometimes for mission projects with college students, sometimes for Passion events, and sometimes just to explore the city. We have friends who live throughout London, so we've been able to see the city through the eyes of its residents as well. We've recorded music at Abbey Road Studios. I've gotten a behind-the-scenes look at Parliament. We've done Passion events at Eventim Apollo and SSE Arena, Wembley.

Having spent so much time in London, Shelley and I would say we know the city pretty well because over the years we've been dividing it up and slicing it up and taking little bite-sized chunks of it so we can taste and see the city. We haven't exhausted everything there is to know about this city—not even close—yet if you'd ask us if we know London, we'd say yes. We don't simply know facts about the city. We've done the deep dive. We've investigated. We've explored. We've examined and studied and searched and found.

Do you realize we can know Almighty God this way? Can we just wrap our heads around this truth?

The invitation is staggering. Yet it's not simply an invitation to know more facts about the Almighty. Shelley and I could have learned a tremendous amount about the city of London from reading books and talking with others. But that's far different from being there in person.

There is a God of infinite greatness, and He has invited you to know Him deeply and closely and richly. The invitation is to sit with Him. To experience Him for yourself. To be in His presence. When you realize the magnitude of this possibility, you see there is nothing in your life more valuable or rewarding than your full-on pursuit of knowing Him.

That's important because one of the strongest things we can do to prevent the Enemy from sitting at our table is to be completely transfixed on the Host who is sitting at our table with us. Oh sure, we know the Enemy is out there. He's prowling around like an old roaring lion, looking for someone to devour. Yet our gaze is transfixed firmly on the God of glory. We're captivated by who He is and all the goodness He has for us. We win the battle for our mind by focusing firmly on Jesus.

SPEECHLESS AT THE BEAUTY

To truly know God, you have to learn to linger with Him.

My father-in-law is one of the most important men in my life. He is a legend to me and to everyone who knows him, but he is a fast mover. When Shelley and I first started dating, we would go out for meals with her parents. The food would come, and we'd start chatting. I'd still be in the middle of eating, but when I'd look over to her dad's plate, it was empty. I'd think, *I know that plate had food on it just forty-five seconds ago.* I decided to set a goal that just once I would eat all of my food before he did. As soon as my plate was on the table, no more conversation. I'd eat as quickly as possible. But I would look up, and, sure enough, her dad was already done!

I had learned to pick up the pace by the time we joined Shelley's mom and dad on a trip through northwest Canada after we were married. We eventually arrived on Victoria Island, where we planned to visit the Butchart Gardens, often considered one of the wonders of the world. I was prepared for a full day of taking in the wonder, but then again, Shelley's dad moves fast.

Guess how much time we spent there. All day? Half the day? Nope, we spent a total of twenty-seven minutes at the Butchart Gardens. And eight of those minutes involved getting ice cream. Shelley's dad had a video camera rolling the whole time as we briskly trekked through the gardens.

As soon as we got our ice cream, he asked, "All right, y'all ready? Let's go."

We said, "No, we just got here. We want to enjoy this amazing place."

He said, "But we have it all on tape. So when we get home we can watch the Butchart Gardens on TV!"

We were in too big of a rush to linger.

Lingering with the Almighty is the best defense against the Enemy who's trying to get at your table. You stop looking at the Enemy and you start looking at God. Sure, there is strategy in knowing the Enemy's tactics, in learning how to keep the Enemy from sitting down. Yet there is even greater strategy in exchanging the defensive for the offensive, the negative for the positive. As we wholeheartedly focus on God and seek His face (Psalm 27:8), great things happen. Yes, wonderful things flood your life when you cultivate an incredible desire to taste and see that the Lord is good (Psalm 34:8).

As C. S. Lewis pointed out, so many people are focused on lessening our desire for worldly things, yet "it would seem that our Lord finds our desires not too strong, but too weak. We are half-hearted creatures, fooling about with drink and sex and ambition when infinite joy is offered us, like an ignorant child who wants to go on making mud pies in a slum because he cannot imagine what is meant by the offer of a holiday at the sea. We are far too easily pleased."[1]

I got a huge dose of this extraordinary invitation to know the Almighty during my college years when a friend and I took a six-week road trip camping in our nation's national parks. I was particularly looking forward to seeing majestic Mount Rainier in the Cascade mountain range near Seattle because I'd studied the glacier-shrouded volcano in a geography class at Georgia State

University. I'd even aced the test. I pretty much knew everything about this mountain.

Or so I thought.

My friend and I drove up the mountain to the highest point we could drive to. We were five thousand feet above sea level, and I figured I'd tell my friend about everything I'd learned in my geography class about the mountain. But when we got out and looked around, I collapsed into an emotional heap of tears. I never got my speech out. The mountain was too huge. Too magnificent. Too brilliant. I was staggered by the mountain. Speechless at its beauty.

The next evening we were camping in Coos Bay, Oregon, and I lay awake staring at the canvas ceiling of the tent, having a conversation with God, asking Him what in the world my response to seeing Mount Rainier had been about. God spoke back into my heart, *Louie, you learned something powerful yesterday. You learned the difference between knowing a lot about something and truly experiencing something up close. You came to the mountain with information. But yesterday you caught a glimpse of revelation.*

That night in the tent, God made it clear to me that I had a choice in life: I could be a person who knew about God, or I could take up the invitation to truly know God. I had a lot of knowledge about God, but what I experienced on Mount Rainier changed everything. I needed to move past the information I knew about God to truly, intimately know God Himself.

That invitation extends to you too.

KNOWING GOD HIMSELF

How does that happen? How do you get to know this Almighty God? You come to Him through the Word of God and the person of Jesus Christ, who said, "Anyone who has seen me has seen the Father" (John 14:9). You come with the help of the Holy Spirit, who guides you into truth (John 14:26). You come to know God by discovering His attributes. As A. W. Tozer said, "An attribute of God is whatever God has in any way revealed as being true of Himself."[2]

The attributes of God can't be exhausted, because God is infinite. Here's an easy example: God is love. This truth is reflected throughout Scripture, but particularly in 1 John. God is not some nebulous force of energy in the cosmos. He's actually a God of personhood, and that includes full will and full emotion. And the thing that drives His will and guides the emotion of God is love. "For God so loved the world that He gave His only begotten Son" (John 3:16 NKJV). "God demonstrates his own love for us in this: While we were still sinners, Christ died for us" (Romans 5:8). When you look into the love of God and study the love of God and meditate on the love of God, then you come to know love as one of God's most extraordinary attributes. You see the heart of God as love. You see love for people as one of His biggest motivators. As you see God as a God of love, you begin to truly know God.

Or think of it this way: if I asked you if you know the game of soccer, chances are really good you'd say yes. I mean, like, anywhere in the world, you'd say yes. Everybody knows soccer (or *football* for those of you outside the US). Okay, but how about if I asked if you know how many players are on the field during a soccer game? Maybe the pool of experience is a little smaller there, but still a lot of people around the world know it's eleven players per team. Okay, but how about if I asked if you know the name of the professional soccer team in Atlanta? Well, a little smaller even still, yet many Americans, if they're inclined toward sports, would have heard of the Atlanta United. But what if I asked if you knew the last year that the Atlanta United won the MLS championship? A little smaller even still. But do you remember the name of the leading scorer of United's 2018 championship season? Can you recall it was the Venezuelan sensation Josef Martinez?

Oh, but we all know soccer, right?!

I mean you can know soccer, and then you can truly *know* soccer. Someone might have watched a soccer game a few times on TV, but someone else has seen every home game, traveled to every away game of their favorite team, and knows the name and jersey number of every player on the Atlanta United. There are so many ways to know something.

The soccer illustration breaks down in the sense that God is Spirit and God has personhood. Knowing God is not like taking a lawn mower apart. So let's put this on an interpersonal scale; let's consider the levels of depth you can explore in knowing another person. If you ask a couple who has been dating for two days what they know and love about each other, the woman might say, "Well, he's tall. Um. And he's sweet. And, uh, he's lots of fun." And that knowledge is true, and it's real, yet it's certainly not everything there is to know about a person.

Ask a couple who has been happily married for twenty years what they know and love about each other, and they'll tell you a completely different story. It'll be a four-hour list. The woman might say, "Well, the way he treats our kids so kindly, the way he looks when he comes home after a run, the way he's patient with his in-laws, the way he's friendly with everybody he meets, the way he has a quick wit, the way he can field every difficult emotion I've ever had, the way he provides for our family, the way he doesn't run out the door after we've had an argument, the way we talk about our faith together. I love this person, not because I read his résumé or can give a four-second summary of who he is, but because we have been in close contact every day of our lives for the past twenty years. I know his traits. I know his mannerisms. I know his character. I know his thoughts. I know his actions. I know what he cares about. I know his heart."

When it comes to knowing God, He invites you not to settle for surface knowledge. He invites you to a deep and personal knowledge of Him where you can explore His grace, His love, His mercy, His immensity, His purity, His holiness, and His omnipotence. You can know how He helps you. How He cares for you. How He provides for you. How He never fails you. How He works things out for your good. How He's full of wisdom. How He's rich in counsel. How He never changes. How He is always everywhere, yet can love you individually. How He's full of justice. How God is kind. How God is gracious. How God is infinitely beautiful and powerful and glorious.

God wants to be known by you, and you can know as much about Him as you have the appetite and desire to know.

GLIMPSES OF GOD

Let's look at two of God's attributes in depth. These attributes aren't all God is, but they'll whet your appetite to know more about Him. And getting to know your Shepherd in this way will help you not give the Enemy a seat at your table.

First, God is holy, and second, God is full of glory. These two attributes are neighbors in the package of truth that we know of God. They're in proximity to each other a lot as they're presented in Scripture and in the person of Jesus Christ.

Okay, God is holy. What does that mean, why should that matter to you, and why would you want to know more about the holiness of God? God is full of glory. Same questions. You can see God's glory on display throughout the universe, yet what difference does it make to you and me to know more about God's glory?

Let's spring off of Isaiah 6, the passage we looked at in the last chapter. We learned how the prophet saw a vision of God and how Isaiah responded by acknowledging his humanity and receiving the mercy of God. Isaiah's guilt was taken away by the live coal. But let's go further into that same text, because there was plenty we skipped over initially. Namely, that God gave Isaiah revelation not just about Himself but *into* Himself. In the text, God is shown as seated on a magnificent throne. He is high and exalted, and the train of His robe fills the temple. Six-winged angels called seraphim are flying above Him, and the seraphim are covering their faces and feet with sets of wings as they fly. They're calling out, "Holy, holy, holy is the LORD Almighty; the whole earth is full of his glory" (Isaiah 6:3).

This passage gives us a very personal glimpse of God. We see similar glimpses in the books of Revelation and Ezekiel. These glimpses are small peeks into heaven where these amazing spirit beings, angels, are simply blown away by God—they are so awed that they can't even look at Him. In honor of Him they cover their feet. And what attribute of God do these angels call out? They're not calling, "Strong, strong, strong." They're not calling, "Faithful, faithful, faithful." They're not calling, "Transcendent, transcendent, transcendent." They're not calling, "Immutable, immutable, immutable." Even though God is all those things and more, the angels have a laser-like focus. They're not tripping up on words. They're not trying to debate theological concepts. They're not searching their Bible software for an inspirational quote. No. They camp on the holiness of God. They're calling, "Holy, holy, holy."

What is holiness? The angels are directing us to the perfection of God, the purity of God, the sinlessness of God. But even those words don't fully convey what holiness is. The word *holy* comes from the Hebrew word *qadash* (pronounced *kaw-dash*). The word conveys two closely related concepts: "sacred" and "set apart."[3] That's what the angels are crying out: "You are sacred and You are set apart! You are sacred and set apart! You are sacred and set apart!"

When we say, "set apart," that means God is in His own league. He's on His own playing field. There's nothing and no one like Him. So in light of that, when you say, "I want to put the Lord first in my heart," that's right on. God can't be relegated to second or third or fourth place. Whether we acknowledge it or not, He is always first, tops, the winner, and He's uniquely in that position. He isn't running a race with anybody else, and He didn't beat out Jo-Jo at the tape with a lean. Jo-Jo isn't even in the same race. No one is in that race. Nothing is in that race. God is holy, sacred, and set apart. In Exodus 15, which includes the first song of praise after the deliverance of the Israelites from Egypt, we find this lyric in verse 11: "Who is like you—majestic in holiness, awesome in glory, working wonders?" That's our God.

What is God's glory about? We think of glory as fame, or the glory of a city, or making it to the cover of a magazine. But that's tinfoil praise. God's glory is far different. God's glory isn't fleeting. His glory isn't measured in a headline. The Hebrew word for glory is *kabod*, again conveying two concepts: "weight" and "worth."[4] God has incalculable substance and incalculable value. He is full of magnitude and He is priceless. That is God's glory.

In the Hebrew, if a word or superlative is repeated, it essentially doubles in emphasis. Very few times in Scripture is a word or superlative tripled for emphasis. In Isaiah 6, the idea is this: "God, You are sacred and set apart. Your weight and Your worth can't be measured. Times all that again, and times all that again. God, You are not only *holy* . . .

"You are *holy, holy, holy!*"

CLIMB HIGH ON THE MOUNTAIN

The choice to know God more fully is yours. Thanks to Jesus, there are no barriers to you knowing God. It wasn't always that way. In the Old Testament, there were limits. People had to look ahead in faith, believing that the barriers sin created between them and God would one day be broken down through the work of a Savior.

Jesus made a way for us to come into the presence of God. To actually know Him without limit. Paul described this in

GOD HAS INCALCULABLE SUBSTANCE AND INCALCULABLE VALUE. HE IS FULL OF MAGNITUDE AND HE IS PRICELESS. THAT IS GOD'S GLORY.

2 Corinthians 3. The ministry of God used to be written on stone tablets, but now that ministry is written on our hearts. Paul went on to say, "Therefore, since we have such a hope, we are very bold. We are not like Moses, who would put a veil over his face to prevent the Israelites from seeing the end of what was passing away" (vv. 12–13). The result now is that we all, with unveiled faces, behold the Lord's glory, and we're being transformed into His image. The cross and the Spirit have brought us freedom. And what is this freedom? To come boldly into His presence. To come as high as we want on the mountain of God.

That's what Christ has done for us. When angels announced His birth, they said, "Glory to God in the highest" (Luke 2:14). The greatest weight and the greatest value have come to earth in Christ. It's such a staggering truth for us today. Jesus opened the way for us to come into the very presence of "holy, holy, holy" God. When Jesus died, "the veil of the temple was torn in two from top to bottom" (Matthew 27:51 NASB). Thanks to Jesus, the separation between God and man does not need to exist anymore. We have access to the Father. Hebrews 10:19–20 lays this out for us explicitly: "We have confidence to enter the Most Holy Place by the blood of Jesus, by a new and living way opened for us through the curtain, that is, his body."

God invites us to climb all the way up His mountain, yet it's far too easy to stand with a pinch of dust's worth of understanding at the base. Your invitation is to climb higher, to go all the way up. As you climb the mountain you find God has infinite power. Infinite love. Infinite beauty. Infinite majesty. Saint Augustine said, "Thou hast made us for Thyself and our hearts are restless till they rest in Thee."[5]

So, you want to know how to keep the Enemy away from your table? Hike up the mountain of God. Sense some of the weight of the worth of His majesty. In the process you will be changed. Scripture clearly tells us that we become what we worship (Psalm 115:8). When we set our gaze on the Almighty, we change into the likeness of the One who has captivated our souls. And we reflect His glory.

SHINING IN THE STRUGGLE

Remember the truth we saw earlier in Psalm 34:5: "Those who look to him are radiant"? When you set your gaze on Jesus, your countenance changes. Literally. Hope begins to shine in your eyes. A smile emerges where there was once a downturned expression. So can you see it? You're sitting with your King in the middle of the conflict. Your enemies have ringside seats. God has moved them from the upper deck and given them a close-up vantage point. What do they see? Do they see you wilting under the pressure or glaring back at them? No, they see you glowing as you stare into the face of majesty.

Wow! This gets us to the heart of the question—*Why put the table in the middle of the enemies?* Because the story we're in is about the greatness of our God. We get the benefits of being led by the Good Shepherd. But Jesus gets the glory as being the greatest Shepherd of all.

God's glory matters more than anything. If people don't know how great and gracious and good He is, how will they not choose something of lesser value? How will they know He's better than everything else if they don't see Him on display in someone like you? I'm soberly reminded of the twenty-one martyrs who were executed while kneeling at the edge of the Mediterranean Sea in Libya a few years ago simply for being Christians.[6] Brazen, their captors ruthlessly snuffed out their lives. Yet only eternity will know the impact of the radiant countenance they displayed as they worshipped the Almighty in the face of death. Surely their captors wondered, *What kind of men are these who sing of heaven when the knife blade is coming their way?*

The table is in the presence of the enemies because God wants you to know that you'll always have enough for every moment, every struggle. He'll sustain you in every dark night. And God wants the enemies to watch you shine. Why? Because in time they will stop gawking at you and turn their attention to the One who has the ability to keep your face beaming (Romans 14:11; Philippians 2:10–11).

Lastly, the table is in the presence of your enemies so they can hear your song. With your eyes locked on Jesus, your worship will be uninterrupted. And your worship will become your weapon. Not only will God be exalted, but chains will break as you fight with this declaration: *It may look like I'm surrounded, but I'm surrounded by You, Jesus.* Everything shifts when you exchange a teacup-sized knowledge of God for an oceanic understanding of who He is.

It will be hard for the Enemy to crowd in on your newfound relationship with God. How do you win the battle for your mind? Keep your mind on Christ. Period. There's no way the Enemy will get a seat at your table.

TEN

THE GARDEN OF
YOUR MIND

Shelley and I regularly take our dog London to an off-leash dog park. She has a terrific time there, running and jumping and playing with the other dogs, and it's a great time for us too.

But it's not all fun and games. There's a culvert in the park with a drainage pipe that comes out from under some buildings. London loves to dart into the drainage pipe. That's a big no-no. The pipe is maybe two feet in diameter, and she jets up in there farther than we can see. We have no idea what's up there other than scary darkness. The pipe is off-limits for London. We've made that clear to her.

London doesn't go in there all the time. Usually we go to the park, and it's just business as usual. Lots of fun with Mom and Dad. But other days, as soon as we get to the dog park, we let her out of the car and it's like you can see London's doggy-mind immediately engage in a battle. I don't know exactly what our dog thinks, but I bet it's something like this: *Hmm. Mom and Dad say I can't go into the pipe. I come out with wet and muddy feet, and I know they don't like that. There might be something up in the pipe that will bite my nose. I know it's not where I'm supposed to go, but . . . it's such an adventure to go up there. Maybe just this once. I'm going to watch them closely to see when they're looking the other way.*

And immediately when we do, *bam*, she's gone. Down the hill. Off she runs like a flash, bent on destruction. Her mind is set on the pipe. Her mind just can't get off that one idea.

Have you ever been stuck in a moment like that yourself?

As this book closes, maybe you're still stuck with a thought or an attitude. You're burdened down with a faulty concept of who you are, or maybe you can't seem to break free from a gripping temptation. You know what God wants for you, yet it's difficult to get your mind off the path that leads to less.

Here's the fact: the battle for your life is fought and won in your mind. God wants you to take control of your mind, in Jesus' name, through the power of His Holy Spirit. You can *think* your way into changing your life for good. That's what we've been talking about in this whole book. God is in the story with us, and because He's in the story with us, we're ultimately in a story of victory. Yet we can get sidetracked and tripped up along the way. We can give the Enemy a seat at our table. But we don't need to.

Romans 8:6 gives a great summary of how we don't need to let the Enemy sit down. In the New American Standard Bible, the verse says, "For the mind set on the flesh is death, but the mind set on the Spirit is life and peace." I love the wording there. Other translations use the phrasing "controlled" or "governed," as in "The mind governed by the flesh is death, but the mind governed by the Spirit is life and peace." But I like the imagery of a mindset on the Spirit. We can have a new mindset, with a new way of seeing ourselves and a new way of thinking about life.

So how do we set our minds on what the Spirit desires?

THE MINDSET THAT LEADS TO LIFE

We need the mindset that leads to life, and I want you to know that your mindset can be different. Your thoughts can be different, and your life can be different because your mind is set on Christ. God is with you. He is on your side. He has established a beachhead of victory through Christ. But the rest is up to you.

How does this all work in actual life? The way you go about stopping the Enemy from sitting at your table is by winning the battle for your mind. Winning the mind battle means replacing

I AM DISPATCHED BY THE HOLY SPIRIT, ON KINGDOM ASSIGNMENTS, TO BE LIGHT IN A DARKENED WORLD, SO OTHERS CAN SEE JESUS.

---

old, harmful thoughts with new, life-giving thoughts. The thinking of these new thoughts will result in doing different things—changed behavior. Victory begins in the mind. One of the big ways to gain victory in your mind is to think less about the Devil or about the evil you're trying to avoid and to think more about God and the truth you're aiming to embrace. One of the most powerful tools at your disposal is the ability to memorize Scripture.

Imagine that your mind is a garden. Seeds can float in on the wind or be dropped by birds or be scattered in your garden by any number of things. But you as the gardener are responsible for what grows there. You have the power to water the good seeds and cultivate the good seeds and pull out any weeds that come from seeds you don't want.

How do you cultivate, weed, and water the garden of your mind? Romans 12:2 says, "Do not conform to the pattern of this world, but be transformed by the renewing of your mind. Then you will be able to test and approve what God's will is—his good, pleasing and perfect will." Whatever you give shelter and sustenance to in your mind is ultimately what will grow in your garden. You're going to reap what you sow.

The way you renew your mind is to wrap your thoughts around Scripture. You can take control of what you think about. You deliberately plant the good seeds / thoughts of God in your mind. As these thoughts take root and grow, they will help remove the destructive weeds that the Enemy tries to plant in your mind.

What follows are seven seeds from God. Wait—don't close this book before it's finished because you're positive that planting seven new truths in your thinking is just too much for you. You can do this! It will take time, but you *can change your mind and, thus, change your life.*

My encouragement to you is to start small. Realigning your thinking with God's thinking is a process. So take one step at a time. Take one thought each day. Dwell on that thought and memorize the scripture. By the end of the week, you'll be well on your way to cultivating the garden of your mind. Or maybe you just want to take one thought and verse each week for seven weeks. Either way, plant and begin to cultivate these seven thoughts in your mind now. Personalize these statements for yourself, and memorize these verses.

1. I am in God's story.

The story of who you are is part of God's larger story. The story is bigger than you. Ultimately, the story is not about you. You have been invited into the story of God's great glory and grace. It's all about Him. But you have a seat at His table.

Before you were formed in your mother's womb, God knew you. Jesus the Good Shepherd guides you always, and the Lord makes firm the steps of those who delight in Him (Psalm 37:23).

So plant this thought in your mind by memorizing this verse: "'I know the plans I have for you,' declares the LORD, 'plans to prosper you and not to harm you, plans to give you hope and a future'" (Jeremiah 29:11).

You matter to God. But ultimate meaning won't come from putting the spotlight on you. Your life will have the greatest significance when you choose to make it about the One who welcomes you into His never-ending story.

2. I am fearfully and wonderfully made.

You weren't born by a random act of the cosmos. God made you with intention, and God made you wonderfully. God has redeemed you and knows your name (Isaiah 43:1).

So plant this thought by memorizing this verse: "You created my inmost being; you knit me together in my mother's womb. I praise you because I am fearfully and wonderfully made; your works are wonderful, I know that full well" (Psalm 139:13–14).

You are not the maker. You are made. God is not created in your image, how you might think He should be. You are created in His. He decided that He wanted you in His universe. He imagined and fashioned you. You are not accidental. Nor incidental. You are divinely crafted.

Plant this seed every day. In time, you'll have an oak providing shade for you and those around you. You'll begin to believe that you are who God says you are. Unique. Special. Valuable.

3. My life has purpose.

You were born for a noble reason. God has good things for you to do. He has called you to live for what matters.

So plant this thought by memorizing this verse: "We are God's handiwork, created in Christ Jesus to do good works, which God prepared in advance for us to do" (Ephesians 2:10).

Random things are random. Evolved things are void of specific meaning. But created things have purpose. There is just one you. You have a unique calling, a reason for being. Something to do in God's great story that is important and needed.

Don't buy into the lie that you are expendable. You're not. God put you on earth for a purpose. Your life matters, to Him and to those He is positioning you to serve.

4. The cross has the final word.

The work Jesus did on the cross defines your life. It gives you victory over death. You are identified with Christ. You are a brand-new creation. You are not unwanted, unlovely, or worthless. You are wanted by God, made in the image of God, and worthy of Christ's love because He has chosen to place worth upon you. Your identity was born in the death, burial, and resurrection of Christ.

Don't let anyone try to convince you of anything that wasn't demonstrated to you when Christ gave His life for you. You are forgiven. Made right. You are holy in Christ. You are born into a new family. Woven into divine plans and purposes. Your guilt is gone. You are free.

So plant this thought by memorizing this verse: "If anyone is in Christ, he is a new creation. The old has passed away. Behold, the new has come!" (2 Corinthians 5:17 BSB).

5. I serve at the pleasure of the King.

The work of Jesus transforms your work. You don't merely work at a job. You serve Jesus Christ, the King of kings.

In light of this truth, here is a new personal vision statement, one you can remind yourself of each day: *I am dispatched by the Holy Spirit, on kingdom assignments, to be light in a darkened world, so others can see Jesus.*

Plant this thought by memorizing this verse: "You are a chosen people, a royal priesthood, a holy nation, God's special possession, that you may declare the praises of him who called you out of darkness into his wonderful light" (1 Peter 2:9).

6. Jesus is Lord, and Jesus is my Lord.

Your God is stronger than anything, higher than anything, and worthy of all praise. Your God is the Great

King. His kingdom is forever; His plans are unassailable and sure.

Plant this thought by memorizing this verse: "God exalted him to the highest place and gave him the name that is above every name, that at the name of Jesus every knee should bow, in heaven and on earth and under the earth, and every tongue acknowledge that Jesus Christ is Lord, to the glory of God the Father" (Philippians 2:9–11).

7. **My God turns evil into good.**

Life doesn't always work out as you hope. You're living on a broken planet. But no circumstance can hinder the seeds we've just discussed from being cultivated in your mind. No hardship or disappointment or disease or divorce or darkness or desert can stunt the growth of godly thoughts from becoming mighty trees in your way of thinking.

So plant this in your mind: "We know that God causes all things to work together for good to those who love God, to those who are called according to His purpose" (Romans 8:28 NASB).

Start there. God has spoken these truths in His Word. Now it's up to you to plant these truths in your mind, and keep tilling them and nurturing them until the Word takes root and grows and produces a crop.

Let the pictures we've drawn illuminate truth for you: the garden is your mind, where you're growing a transformed person by planting God's Word. That person is sitting at the table, the place of fellowship with the Good Shepherd, where you don't want to give the Devil a seat; you want to enjoy the meal with your Lord. The mountain represents the grandeur of the Lord Himself, and your privilege is to ascend higher and higher in getting to know Him. All these pictures are about the deep and deepening relationship with the God of the universe that you are invited into. Don't be scared. Jesus the Good Shepherd guides you every step of the way.

A CONTINUOUS LEAN

Scripture is clear: Jesus lives in you, and when Jesus lives in you, your slate is clean. You are set free from condemnation, and you are given a new life and placed into a new family. You have a relationship with God through Jesus. Christ's work on the cross got you out of death, so now your life can be lived fully surrendered to Him. You are alive in the Spirit, alive by the Spirit, alive for Christ, alive in Christ, to live the life of Christ so that He might be glorified. This is not a negotiation. This is a call to surrender completely to Jesus. You are completely open, completely available to Him. He has given you a new identity. Your call is to make Him known in the world.

I don't know about you, but I want to daily set my mind and heart on Christ. I want to constantly fill my mind with Scripture. I don't want to waste any time. I don't want to get off track. I don't want to give the Enemy a seat at my table. I want to set my mind on the Spirit and daily surrender to Him. God has made a way for you and me, and it's not by having our own way. It's by entering into the process of making Christ known in the world.

I know that I want God to move in a supernatural way in my life. I don't want to get to the end of my days and look back to see a cookie-cutter life that looks like what society says a normal life should be. I don't want average. I don't want the easiest path. I want to know God intimately, deeply. And I want my life to defy human explanation.

I'm thinking this is the life you want too. This kind of life can be yours. One that's dependent fully on the power of the Holy Spirit. And it's activated by you stepping forward in faith. Too often we want to see miracles first, before we take a step. We're like, "Okay God, do something great, and then I'll take the step. Give me all the right words first, and then I'll take the microphone. Give me all the money first, and then I'll start what You've called me to do. Provide the spouse I need, and then I'll step into the unknown." But the fullness of the life that Jesus provides becomes evident to us often when we move, when we act on His leading, when we open our mouths and speak. The steps we take in faith activate the power of the Spirit.

That's your call today.

Don't give the Enemy a seat at your table. You can win the battle for your mind. Don't give in to sin, despair, or darkness. Take every thought captive. Bind every thought in Jesus' name that doesn't come from God. Fill your mind with the goodness and richness of Scripture. Memorize Scripture, and become the DJ of your mind, letting thoughts of God consistently fill your heart and life. Surrender your life completely to Jesus. He will lead you to green pastures and quiet waters. He will lead you through dark valleys, but you don't ever need to fear. You will not be in want, because Jesus will restore your soul. Jesus will lead you to a table in the presence of your enemies, but there's nothing to worry about, because your head is dripping with anointing, your cup overflows with abundance, and goodness and mercy are following you all the days of your life.

The Good Shepherd is sitting at your table. Jesus has invited you to all the abundance He offers. It's a meal for the two of you. He Himself is the feast.

ACKNOWLEDGMENTS

Every book takes a journey, and, in this case, that journey would not have been completed without a village. Shelley and I are so blessed to be part of the best team in the world at Passion, and to have incredible partners in HarperCollins Christian Publishing and the W Publishing Group.

I'm indebted to my writing partner, Marcus Brotherton, an award-winning author in his own right. Thank you, Marcus, for helping shape this story and for giving added voice to the messages that are woven together in this book. I admire your writing skill yet equally appreciate your desire to see the Holy Spirit connect the truths of God's Word with people's hearts in a transformational way.

This book was created in partnership with Kevin Marks, the head of our Passion Publishing team and a legend in Christian publishing. I love that you are literally on the other side of the wall between our offices, leading with steady wisdom and navigating so well the partnership we share with HCCP. Thank you, also, to Emily Floyd, our project manager, and to Rachelle Legentus, our marketing manager.

I'm so grateful for everyone at HarperCollins Christian Publishing, beginning with Mark Schoenwald, Don Jacobson (who published my very first book and recently joined HCCP), and Damon Reiss (who leads the team at W Publishing). I'm honored to work alongside the W Publishing team: Kyle Olund, Meaghan Porter, Kristen Paige Andrews, Caren Wolfe, Laura Askvig, Allison Carter, and the rest of this outstanding team.

My personal team at Passion is exceptional, providing writing/editing assistance, creative advice, marketing and social media awareness, constant encouragement, and so much more. I could not have completed this project without the help of my executive project manager and our chief counsel, Sue Graddy, as well as my direct support team: Ana Munoz, Jake Daghe, Britt Adams, and Macie Vance.

Shelley and I are part of an amazing family of creatives, strategists, artists, pastors, and builders at Passion. Together they help cultivate and lead a robust ecosystem that enables books like this one to reach people around the world.

The cover design is the brilliant handiwork of Passion Design leader Leighton Ching, along with supporting online design by Chandler Saunders, with Kaitlin Randolph as project manager.

I'm grateful for Misty Paige, Courtney McCormick, and Justine Simon, who are giving leadership to Passion Resources in this season and helping so many people find their way to this book.

In addition, Joe Gannon, Kevin Stacy, James Vore, and Lindsey Williams manage our storytelling and marketing channels with the belief that many lives will be touched and encouraged by this message.

Shelley and I are grateful for each of you and treasure the opportunity we have to make much of God together.

NOTES

CHAPTER 2: THE TWENTY-THIRD PSALM—REMIX

1. For their full story, see Katherine and Jay's books: Katherine and Jay Wolf, *Suffer Strong* (Nashville: Zondervan, 2020) and *Hope Heals* (Nashville: Zondervan, 2016).

CHAPTER 3: MIND IF I SIT DOWN?

1. I've shared this story more than once, so you might have heard it before. But it's vital to the heart of the message in this book, the message we face so many times without even realizing it, which is why I share it again here.

CHAPTER 6: FREEDOM REVOLUTION

1. "What Happens If You Fall into Quicksand?," produced by What If?, in conjunction with Underknown and Ontario Creates, July 24, 2019, https://www.youtube.com/watch?v=jYlZyO62V7A.

2. For a helpful, quick study of the word *saint*, see the video "Is Every Christian a Saint?" by John Piper, on his *Desiring God* blog, June 22, 2017, https://www.desiringgod.org/labs/is-every-christian-a-saint.

3. Jack May, "Which Is London's Deepest Tube Station?," City Monitor, April 5, 2017, https://www.citymetric.com/transport /which-london-s-deepest-tube-station-2938.

4. The illustration is also found in Priscilla Shirer, *Awaken: 90 Days with the God Who Speaks* (Nashville: B&H Books, 2017), Day 51.

CHAPTER 7: TAKE EVERY THOUGHT CAPTIVE

1. Dave Roos, "D-Day: Facts on the Epic 1944 Invasion That Changed the Course of WWII," History, last updated June 4, 2020, https://www.history.com/news/d-day-normandy-wwii-facts.

CHAPTER 9: STAGGERED BY THE MOUNTAIN

1. C. S. Lewis, *The Weight of Glory* (San Francisco: HarperCollins, 2001), 25–26.

2. A. W. Tozer, *Knowledge of the Holy*, repr. ed. (New York: HarperOne, 2009), 13.

3. James Strong, *Strong's Exhaustive Concordance of the Bible* (Nashville: Thomas Nelson, 2009), 6942.

4. Strong, 3519.

5. Augustine, *Confessions*, trans. F. J. Sheed, 2nd ed. (Indianapolis: Hackett, 2006), 1.1.1.

6. David D. Kirkpatrick and Rukmini Callimachi, "Islamic State Video Shows Beheadings of Egyptian Christians in Libya," *New York Times*, February 15, 2015, https://www.nytimes.com/2015 /02/16/world/middleeast/islamic-state-video-beheadings-of-21 -egyptian-christians.html.

ABOUT THE AUTHOR

Louie Giglio is pastor of Passion City Church and original visionary of the Passion movement, which exists to call a generation to leverage their lives for the fame of Jesus.

Since 1997, Passion Conferences has gathered collegiate-aged young people in events across the US and around the world. Most recently, Passion hosted over 700,000 people from over 150 countries online at Passion 2021.

Louie is the national-bestselling author of over a dozen books, including his newest release, *Don't Give the Enemy a Seat at Your Table,* as well as *Goliath Must Fall, Indescribable: 100 Devotions About God & Science, The Comeback, The Air I Breathe, I Am Not But I Know I Am,* and others. As a communicator, Louie is widely known for messages like Indescribable and How Great is Our God.

An Atlanta native and graduate of Georgia State University,

Louie has done post-graduate work at Baylor University and holds a master's degree from Southwestern Baptist Theological Seminary. Louie and his wife, Shelley, make their home in Atlanta.

Video Study for Your
Church or Small Group

If you've enjoyed this book, now you can go deeper with the companion video Bible study!

In this six-session study, Louie Giglio helps you apply the principles in *Don't Give the Enemy a Seat at Your Table* to your life. The study guide includes video notes, group discussion questions, and personal study materials for in between sessions.

Study Guide
9780310134244

DVD with
Free Streaming Access
9780310134268

Available now at your favorite bookstore,
or streaming video on StudyGateway.com.

passion publishing   W Publishing Group